COMMANDOS

BEHIND ENEMY LINES

PRIMA'S OFFICIAL STRATEGY GUIDE

COMMANDOS™

BEHIND ENEMY LINES

PRIMA'S OFFICIAL STRATEGY GUIDE

MICHAEL KNIGHT

PRIMA PUBLISHING
Rocklin, California
(916) 632-4400
www.primagames.com

PRIMA The Prima logo and Prima Publishing® are registered trademarks Prima Communications, Inc.

Project Editor: Sara E. Wilson
Product Manager: Stacy DeFoe

Important:
Prima Publishing has made every effort to determine that the information contained in this book is accurate. However, the publisher makes no warranty, either expressed or implied, as to the accuracy, effectiveness, or completeness of the material in this book; nor does the publisher assume liability for damages, either incidental or consequential, that may result from using the information in this book. The publisher cannot provide information regarding game play, hints and strategies, or problems with hardware or software. Questions should be directed to the support numbers provided by the game and device manufacturers in their documentation. Some game tricks require precise timing and may require repeated attempts before the desired result is achieved.

ISBN: 7615-1745-6
Library of Congress Catalog Card Number: 98-66748
Printed in the United States of America

98 99 00 01 BB 10 9 8 7 6 5 4 3

CONTENTS

INTRODUCTION

The smaller the unit, the better its performance.

—T.E. Lawrence (a.k.a. "Lawrence of Arabia")

WELCOME TO WORLD WAR II

During World War II, millions of men and women took an active role in the fighting. Armies comprising tens of thousands of soldiers battled across the European continent. Their might and firepower changed the landscape and devastated entire cities. Never before had human hands wrought such destruction.

The warring powers also employed small units that could accomplish what entire armies could not. During the war, the British Army created the "Commandos" units to take the war to the Germans while the British recovered from the evacuation at Dunkirk. Their missions consisted primarily of infiltration and sabotage. The Commandos didn't win the war for the Allies, but they greatly improved British morale during desperate times. In many cases, the Commandos preceded the regular army, sowing chaos and confusion among the enemy before an Allied attack.

In *COMMANDOS™: Behind Enemy Lines*, you take command of such a unit. However, although some of your missions are based on historical actions, most have a cinematic flair. This isn't surprising. Like myself, the game developers grew up watching war movies, and you'll detect this Hollywood influence throughout the game. Several missions resemble movies such as *The Dirty Dozen*, *Force 10 from Navarone*, and *Where Eagles Dare*, among others. Your missions take you from Norway to North Africa and then back to Europe.

Unlike other real-time strategy games, *COMMANDOS* requires careful planning. Instead of building lots and lots of units with powerful weapons, you control from two to six men, depending on the mission. Some missions include a machine gun or explosives, but your Commandos will often favor knives or other silent weapons. Stealth and cunning are vital to completing all the missions.

In the planning scene from *The Dirty Dozen*, Lee Marvin gathers his team around a model of the German headquarters they must destroy. The soldiers must perform their tasks in a certain order, so Marvin creates a mnemonic device, a rhyme something like, "One, Smith takes out the gun. Two, Jones pulls the fuse. . . ." *COMMANDOS* is similar in that you must perform certain tasks in a specific order. In missions with many guards in the same area, you must determine which you can kill without alarming the others. The walkthrough chapters include maps showing the order in which you must eliminate enemies.

Your Commandos must work closely together. Each has special skills and abilities. For example, only the Green Beret can move barrels, only the Marine can operate water craft, and only the Sapper can handle explosives. Each is essential, so you must watch over them carefully and keep them safe. If any die, you must start the mission over. You'll need certain Commandos in each mission, and all of them for the final mission.

HOW TO USE THIS GUIDE

This strategy guide will help make you a master Commando. The first chapter covers the game interface, as well as the types of enemies you'll face. Chapter 2 introduces you to each Commando and explains how best to use him. It includes interactive training, using the game's tutorials. Next, in Chapter 3, we cover the strategies and tactics you must know to complete the missions. We refer to many of these in the mission walkthroughs in chapters 4 through 6. Each walkthrough covers one of the three campaigns, taking you step by step through each mission so you can play with the guide open. Finally, you'll find strategies and tactics for multiplayer games in Chapter 7.

We don't mean for the strategies and tactics in this guide to be all-inclusive. Those we present are proven and known to work well. However, you can complete many missions doing things in a different order or by other means. We encourage you to develop a style of your own.

Well, don't just sit there, daylight's burning and the Nazis are taking over the world. Get going!

FOREWORD

COMMANDOS STRATEGY GUIDE

When Pyro Studios developed *Commandos™: Behind Enemy Lines*, it was driven by an admiration for the heroic exploits of these special soldiers in one of the world's darkest hours. Designer Ignacio Perez spent weeks researching the history of the commando ranks of World War II. He also viewed classic WWII films, including *The Dirty Dozen* and *Where Eagles Dare*. His research inspired this loving, painstaking creation, a game based on a glorious history, in a colorful, yet realistic, Hollywood-style portrayal.

COMMANDOS' established international success shows that gamers have embraced this "new, yet old" game: new, because it marries real-time tactical and strategic combat genres with tantalizing puzzle and RPG elements; old, because although it incorporates superb graphics, audio, and multiplayer features, Pyro Studios remembered what's most essential—enjoyable gameplay.

As producer, I had the good fortune to assist the Pyro team in creating this classic. I appreciate their support, and that of my Eidos coworkers and our fans. I can say with confidence that you'll soon see our "Dirty Half-Dozen" again in action behind enemy lines. Thanks for buying the game and this strategy guide. Now go save the world!

— Eric Adams, Producer

CHAPTER 1

BASIC TRAINING

Before exploring the deep, insightful strategies and tactics it takes to complete the three campaigns' 20 missions, let's go over some basics. First, you'll learn how to control your Commandos. Then you'll get a briefing on the enemy with whom you must do battle. Finally, we'll cover the promotion process.

Now get to your first class. Dismissed!

CONTROLLING THE COMMANDOS

Each Commando has unique weapons and abilities, but in this section we discuss only the aspects of control common to all six Commandos. Chapter 2 provides specifics for individual Commandos.

MOVEMENT

You can control each Commando using the mouse alone. Time can be a matter of life and death, however, and adding a few hotkeys can increase your Commandos' speed and efficiency.

But first, let's learn how to move your men. To select a Commando to control, either click on his portrait or press the hotkey corresponding with his name.

COMMANDO HOTKEYS

Commando	Hotkey
Green Beret	1
Sniper	2
Marine	3
Sapper	4
Driver	5
Spy	6

Figure 1-1.
This Commando won't know where to go unless you give him orders.

After selecting a Commando, give him movement orders by placing the cursor over his destination and clicking the mouse. The Commando will walk to the destination, taking the shortest route and moving around obstacles on his own. To pick up the pace, double-click on the destination to make the Commando double-time it to that spot. During many missions, you will want to move around unseen by the enemy. Press [C] to order the Commando to go prone. Then, when you click on a destination, he'll crawl. To stand up again, press [S].

There may be times when you'll want to move more than one Commando. To form a group, click on each Commando's portrait while holding down [Ctrl]. Or hold down the right mouse button and drag a box around the Commandos you wish to group. Then you can order them all to crawl, run, walk, and even shoot. Because all

Figure 1-2.
To make your Commando hit the dirt, press [C] or click on the prone soldier at the top of the screen.

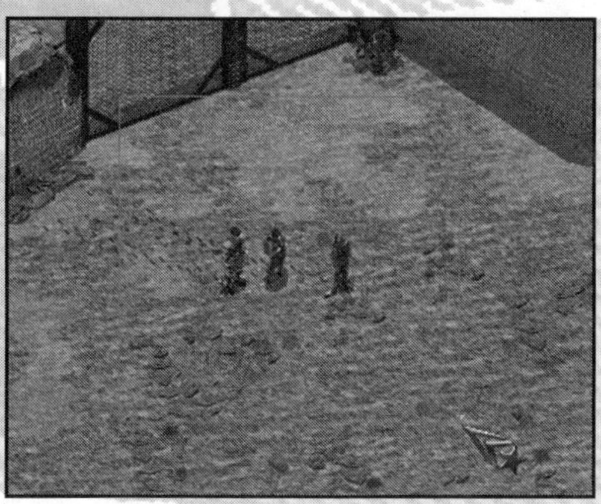

Figure 1-3.
To select a group of Commandos, hold down the right mouse button and drag a box around them.

Commandos carry a pistol, you can order all selected Commandos to fire at the same target—a quick way to kill enemy soldiers.

ACTIONS

Moving is only one of the things you can have your Commandos do. They can perform many other actions, including picking things up, operating or manipulating items, and firing weapons.

Figure 1-4.
Select the hand symbol or press C to order your Commando to pick something up.

Each Commando's knapsack bears a hand symbol. When you click on this, or press H, the cursor becomes a hand within a "prohibited" icon. When you place it over something the Commando can pick up, the prohibited icon vanishes. Not all Commandos can pick up the same things. As a rule, a Commando can pick up only what he can carry and/or operate. For example, the Green Beret can pick up his decoy, dead bodies, and barrels, but not explosives. Only the Sapper can do that.

Manipulating many items you find in the missions requires no skill or ability of your Commandos. If an item can be manipulated, the cursor changes to a hand-pulling-a-lever icon when placed over that item. These include crossing gates, electric power switches, and so forth. This symbol will also appear over ladders. Clicking on a ladder with the lever icon orders your Commando to climb the ladder. Your Commandos may enter and hide in some buildings on the map. If a building is vacant, the lever icon appears over the door when you move the cursor there. To have him leave, click on the Commando's picture on his knapsack.

Each Commando carries different weapons and equipment, but the way you order him to use them is basically the same for all Commandos. Select the item you wish to use by clicking on it in the knapsack or by pressing its hotkey. If that alone doesn't use the item, the cursor will change, waiting for you to designate a target. If

Figure 1-5.
This Commando is targeting the enemy with the pistol. Place the cursor over the enemy and click to fire.

the item is a gun, the cursor turns into crosshairs or a symbol of the weapon, and you'll place it over the target and click to fire. Once he's pulled out a gun (including the grenade), you can no longer give your Commando movement orders. You must first put the weapon away (right-click the mouse), and then give the order to move.

Other items, and even abilities, require the Commando to move closer to the target to use them. You needn't click on a target. If you click on a nontarget, the Commando will only walk to that location and await further orders. (Double-clicking orders the Commando run there, instead.)

TIP

Although you can't follow movement orders when you have a gun or grenade in your hand, this doesn't mean you can't move. For instance, you may want to run after a soldier and shoot him. Place the movement cursor on the target—or past him, if he's moving—and send your Commando to him. While the Commando is moving, you can pull out the weapon and place it over the target. Fire when the target is in range, or at your discretion.

HEALTH

Your Commandos are flesh-and-blood beings who don't react well to being struck by high-velocity pieces of metal. In other words, bullets hurt. Next to each Commando's portrait at the top of the screen is a vertical red bar. When a Commando is shot or otherwise wounded, the bar lowers, reflecting his declining health. When the bar shows no red whatsoever, the Commando is dead, and a skull replaces his portrait. This isn't good: you can't complete a mission unless all your Commandos survive. Now you must play the mission again. That is, you could continue, but when you reach the end, the game won't let you advance to the next mission. One of your Commandos will be designated team medic. He can use the first aid kit on wounded Commandos, including himself, to heal wounds and restore health.

VEHICLES

Many missions feature vehicles of some type. Although only the Driver can operate land vehicles, such as trucks and tanks, the Marine is the only Commando who can row boats or sail other water craft. The other Commandos can climb into and ride in these vehicles, but only the correct operator can make it go.

Your men can't hide in vehicles. When it comes to being spotted, a Commando in a vehicle might as well be out in the open. However, a tank or other armored vehicle will offer your men some protection from enemy fire.

Figure 1-6.
The tank will become your favorite vehicle. All your Commandos can ride in it, protected from your enemies' small arms fire while the Driver guns down them down.

Vehicles move a little differently from Commandos. To drive a vehicle, the operator clicks on a destination. (Double-click to have land vehicles drive fast.) The vehicle will drive directly to the targeted location. If obstacles lie in its path, it will run into them and stop, so steer your vehicles by providing waypoints.

Some vehicles, such as tanks, carry weapons. The operator can fire these by holding down Ctrl so the cursor turns into crosshairs and then clicking on a target to fire at it. Turreted vehicles must wait for their turret to turn and point at the target before firing.

THE ENEMIES

You've learned how to use your Commandos, so let's discuss your opposition and how they operate. You must know your enemy to defeat him.

TYPES OF ENEMY UNITS

COMMANDOS contains a number of different types of enemy units. Each carries out his duty in his own way.

SENTRIES

These soldiers are posted at a specific spot. Although they don't move, they look around and may even turn in place to increase their line of sight. Depending on the importance of what they guard, they may either leave their post if they see or hear your Commandos or just turn in that direction.

Figure 1-7.
Sentries stay in a single spot, but they do look around.

Figure 1-8.
This soldier walks a set path, either back and forth or in a circuit.

SOLDIERS ON WATCH ROUNDS

Unlike the sentries, soldiers on watch rounds will walk a certain route, either back and forth or in a circuit. If they see or hear your men, or if an alarm goes off, they'll leave their route and seek you. If this type of soldier has a view to one of your targets, wait until he turns around and begins walking the other way before carrying out your plans.

PATROLS

Patrols comprise two to five soldiers. The leader is usually armed with a pistol, and the men who follow carry machine guns or rifles. These units are among the game's deadliest, because they're so difficult to take out—especially if you must do it silently. Therefore, find ways to avoid patrols or work around them. If you must elimi-

Figure 1-9.
Patrols can be difficult to kill and carry a lot of firepower.

nate them, kill the soldiers first and leave the leader for last. Your Commandos will fare far better against a pistol than a machine gun.

GUN POSITIONS

These include everything from machine-gun nests to artillery posts. Any can quickly kill your Commandos unless you avoid them or take them out. You can kill machine-gunners as you do regular soldiers; however, some occupied artillery posts must be blown up. Gun positions can't move, but they can aim in all directions to fire at you.

Figure 1-10. If a machine-gun nest spots one of your men, it won't take long for it to kill your Commando.

VEHICLES

Most scenarios contain vehicles that move around. Not all are enemy controlled, but if your Commandos get in their way, some vehicles—trains and boats, for example—can be deadly, nevertheless. Enemy-controlled vehicles can spot just like a soldier and have set routes, like soldiers on watch rounds. They're usually armed with heavy weapons ranging from machine guns to cannons. All are extremely deadly to your men. Because these vehicles are usually armored, you can destroy them only with explosives or grenades.

SIGHT AND SOUND

The enemies in *COMMANDOS* aren't dumb. Neither are they blind or deaf. Each soldier can look around and hear things within a certain radius. To see what a given soldier sees, shift-click on him. Notice that the arc that appears is two shades of green. The soldier will see everything within the closer, brighter area. Within the darker, more distant area, the soldier can see only standing Commandos.

Figure 1-11.
The green arc illustrates what the soldier can see. Shift-click on the soldier to bring up the vision arc.

Your men who are prone or crawling will remain undetected in this zone.

The key to most missions is to keep very quiet. When you use pistols or explosives, the sound carries a certain distance. Soldiers in range of the sound will hear and come looking for you. This isn't always a bad thing. For example, you can use sound to lure a soldier into a trap or away from the watchful eyes of his companions.

The enemy can speak, as well. If he sees you, he'll demand you halt, or just shoot you. If other soldiers can hear this, they may come to investigate. When a soldier sees or hears something that really concerns him, he'll cry out, "Alarm." If he's near a barracks, this will set off an alarm and reinforcements will pour out of the building, ready to kill your men.

The rule of thumb for nearly every mission is to stay quiet and out of sight. Save the explosions and gunplay for the end.

ADVANCEMENT

To complete a mission, you must achieve all its objectives, such as blowing up a radar installation or rescuing a pilot, and then get all your Commandos to safety. Yes, *all*

Figure 1-12.
So how did you do during the mission?

of them! In many games, your units are expendable. Not so here. All must make it through all 20 missions. Any Commando you lose will be needed in at least the final mission, if not several others. There's no time to train replacements. You'll just have to be careful.

At the end of each mission, a debriefing screen will display how many soldiers you killed and how many buildings and vehicles you destroyed. This is just for your information. You receive no points for kills. Whether you killed two soldiers or a hundred, it doesn't affect your award. What matters is the time it took you to complete the mission and the wounds your men sustained. The more quickly you complete the mission, the more points you receive. You're rewarded, as well, for keeping your men healthy: they have little time to recover before going on to the next mission.

During the campaigns, your point totals for each mission accumulate. These points determine your advancement in rank. You begin as a Corporal, but you can become a Field Marshall by the end of the game if you keep your Commandos healthy and complete the missions quickly. Remember, your military career depends on how well you do, and so does your retirement pay.

CHAPTER 2

THE COMMANDOS

In *COMMANDOS*, you control a team of handpicked combat veterans specially trained in small-unit tactics, demolitions, sabotage, and unconventional warfare. As their leader, you must get to know each one well—his strengths, weaknesses, and abilities. Each Commando has a specialty. Only certain Commandos can use some types of weapons or equipment. This chapter acquaints you with the six team members, and includes dossiers, basic tactics, weapons, skills and abilities, and tutorial walkthroughs for each.

The tutorial walkthroughs will help you develop the skills you'll need to complete the missions, and illustrate how to use the mission walkthroughs in chapters 4, 5, and 6. Screenshots show where to find numbered enemy soldiers on the map.

THE GREEN BERET

You'll use the Green Beret more than any other Commando. He's an expert in hand-to-hand combat and can kill more enemies than any other team member. The Green Beret uses brute strength and deception to carry out his assignments.

VITAL STATISTICS

Name: Jerry "Tiny" McHale

Date of Birth: Sept. 17, 1909

Place of Birth: Chicago

Country: USA

Rank: Sergeant

Height: 6 ft. 5 in.

Weight: 220 lbs.

BACKGROUND

1934–37: U.S. Judo champion

1937: Enlists in U.S. Marines

1938: Receives commendation for close-combat skills

1938: Reprimanded for severely beating four men in a New York bar

1939: Condemned to 15 years' hard labor for knocking out superior during training exercise

1940: Sentence commuted for enlisting with Commando Corps

MILITARY RECORD

OPERATION ON THE ISLAND OF VAAGSO

The Green Beret was promoted to sergeant for his heroism: cut off from his unit and without ammunition, he infiltrated a bunker and eliminated 16 enemy soldiers before returning to the Allied lines.

INCURSION AT TMIMI AIRFIELD

He received the Distinguished Service medal for attacking a watchtower with a bayonet while under enemy fire. Despite receiving light wounds in one arm, he eliminated 15 enemy soldiers before his mates could assist him.

SKILLS AND EQUIPMENT

COMBAT KNIFE

The Green Beret's weapon of choice is the Commandos' official knife, the Wilkinson Sword combat knife. It is 177 mm long and made of carbon steel. Press [X] to have him pull it out of his scabbard. Place the "knife" cursor over the enemy you wish to kill, and click. The Green Beret will walk or crawl to the target and take the enemy out. To run to a target, double-click on the target soldier.

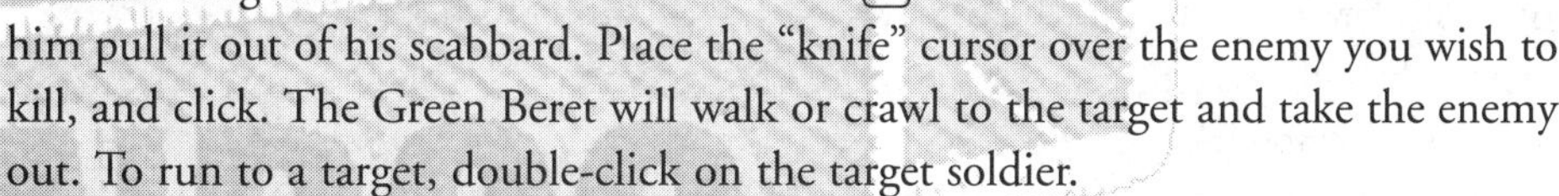

PISTOL

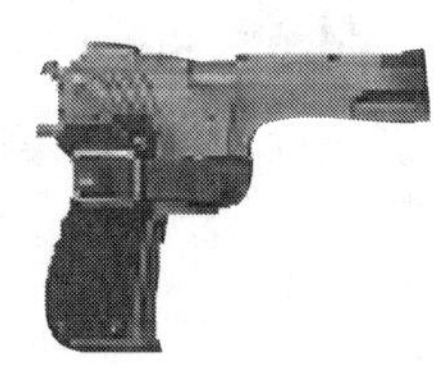

The pistol, a Smith and Wesson W9 9mm pistol with a 10-round clip, is the least-used Commando weapon. To pull the pistol from its holster, press [G]; the cursor will

change to a pistol. Click on the target to fire. It takes three shots to kill an enemy soldier. The pistol never runs out of ammo and you can use it to detonate explosive barrels. The concussion can alert other soldiers to your presence and even cause them to sound an alarm, so use the pistol sparingly.

PICK

The Green Beret's climbing pick allows him to climb cliffs, ridges, and even smooth walls. If a surface is climbable, the cursor will become a pick. Click on the surface to have the Green Beret move over to it and climb. Use the same procedure to descend.

DECOY

This is one of the Green Beret's favorite toys. The decoy is a small acoustical transmitter that makes an unusual noise. Nearby enemy soldiers will hear it and turn toward the decoy, or even walk to it. To place the decoy, press Q, position the Green Beret behind cover, and press I to activate the decoy by remote control. The decoy is a great way to lure enemy soldiers into traps and ambushes. To retrieve a decoy, press H and place the cursor over the decoy to pick it up.

SHOVEL

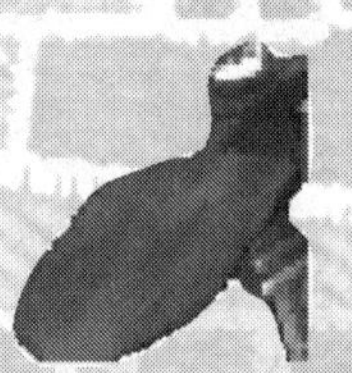

The Green Beret can use the shovel to dig himself into sand or snow to hide. To use the shovel, position the Green Beret on sand or snow, press F, and he'll camouflage himself. Enemy soldiers can walk right over him and not notice. However, if the enemy sees you digging, they'll know where you are even after you're in the hole. To rise up out of the hole, right-click the mouse. When you're hidden, you can't activate or deactivate the decoy.

TIP

A good Green Beret tactic is to lure an enemy to his position with the decoy. Before the enemy arrives, the Green Beret will hide. The enemy will see nothing and maybe even walk right over the hidden Commando. When the enemy looks away, the Green Beret can jump up and knife him.

MOVING BARRELS

The Green Beret is the only Commando strong enough to lift and carry barrels around the map. To do this, place the cursor over a barrel until it becomes a lever. Click and the Green Beret will go over to and pick up the barrel. Right-click the mouse to have him move it and put it down. The barrels are heavy, so the Green Beret can't run while he carries them. Because shooting at these barrels detonates the explosive substances they contain, you can use them as impromptu bombs for blowing up things, including nearby enemies.

CARRYING BODIES

The Green Beret also can pick up bodies of dead soldiers. Press [H] to change the cursor to "pick-up" mode; then click on the body. The Green Beret will walk the body to another place and drop it (right-click). The Spy can carry bodies, as well.

HIDING BODIES IN BARRELS

Often, there are no good places to hide a body. To hide the body in a barrel, have the Green Beret pick up a barrel; then move the cursor over a body until it shows a body-in-a-barrel icon. Click and the Green Beret will drop the barrel onto the body. If he picks the barrel up again, the body remains inside the barrel.

TUTORIAL

The Green Beret begins in the southwest corner of the map. His objective is to kill all six soldiers, blow up the two building mock-ups, and then get to the flag in the northwest corner. [Shift]-click on Soldier 1. The green arc indicates what the

Figure 2-1. The Green Beret must kill all enemies and destroy the two building mock-ups.

soldier is looking at. When he reaches the south end of his route, run after him, carefully staying out of his line of sight, and hide in the snow behind him. To dig a hole to hide in, press [F] and the Green Beret will use the shovel.

The soldier will come back and may look around because he sees the footprints you left in the snow. Take care when walking across snow or sand, because your Commandos will leave footprints behind and alert the enemy to your presence. (You can also use this to lure a guard into a trap or ambush.) The soldier will give up looking for you and continue south. After he passes, right-click to raise the Green Beret from the snow and press [X] to bring out his knife. Place it over the enemy and double-click to order the Green Beret to run after and knife Soldier 1. Although no one can see the body, press [H] and click on the soldier to pick up the body; then carry it behind the rocks where you began the training session. Drop the body with a right-click.

Soldier 2 is patrolling near the wall. We'll use the decoy, now. Place it along the north side of the rock, near where you hid from Soldier 1, by pressing [Q]. Then move around to the south side of the rock. Press [1] to activate the decoy. It will make an unusual sound. When 2 hears it, he'll come to investigate. Sneak around the east side of the rock, approach 2 from behind, and give him the blade. Turn off the decoy (press [I] again), and then pick it up by pressing [H] and then clicking on it.

The concrete wall blocks your path to the rest of the training area. Move to the wall, directly behind Soldier 3. When Patrol 4 walks past him and heads east, place the cursor on the wall until it turns into a pick. Click and the Green Beret will climb the wall. Place the pick on the other side of the wall to climb down. Bring out the knife and kill 3. Then pick up the nearest explosive barrel (press [H]), move the cursor over 3's body, and drop the barrel on the soldier to hide his body. Pick up the barrel again and move it to the south corner of the eastern mock building. Then move back a bit from it and pull out the pistol ([G]). Place the pistol-cursor over the barrel. When the patrol walks near it, click to fire. Each click fires a single bullet. The shot will detonate the barrel, killing the patrol and destroying the building.

Use the pistol sparingly during a mission. Its sound gives away your presence to the enemy, and it can be difficult to kill more than one soldier with it because you must fire three times to kill each enemy. Because enemy soldiers usually are armed with rifles or machine guns, usually they will kill you first. Now pick up the other barrel and move it near the next mock building. Shoot it with the pistol and then run to the flag to end the session. Good job!

THE SNIPER

The Sniper is available in over half the missions. His usefulness is limited, but if he's assigned to a mission, you'll know he is needed to take out enemies from a distance.

VITAL STATISTICS

Name: Sir Francis T. Woolridge, a.k.a. "Duke"

Date of Birth: March 21, 1909

Place of Birth: Sheffield

Country: England

Rank: Soldier

Height: 6 ft. 2 in.

Weight: 180 lbs.

BACKGROUND

1936: Gold Medal in shooting, Munich Olympics

1937: Enlists in the army

1937–39: Stationed in India, stands out as excellent marksman

1940: Joins the Commandos

MILITARY RECORD

AUCHINLECK OFFENSIVE

Receives a military medal after killing the commandant of the German garrison in Narvik. He did so with a single shot at a distance of more than a mile, as the officer inspected his troops' positions.

ADDITIONAL INFO

Descends from a noble family; famous for his steady pulse

Moody; comrades resent his good looks and charm with ladies

Hates alcohol

Deeply resents the Germans for killing his sister in a bomb raid

Cold and calculating

Expert marksman, extremely effective even in situations of great tension

SKILLS AND EQUIPMENT

PRECISION RIFLE

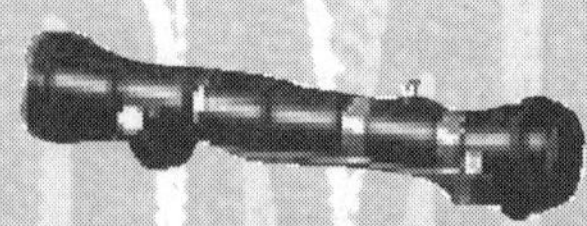

The precision rifle is the main tool of the Sniper's trade. It allows him to kill enemy soldiers from great distances. Press [R] to bring up the rifle. The cursor will change to a reticle view that magnifies anything it's placed over. To kill a target, align the crosshairs over it and click to fire. If the target is out of range or if an obstacle obstructs the line of fire, the sight will turn red, indicating "no shot."

The Sniper's rifle is silent, as well, so you can fire it unnoticed near enemy soldiers. The downside to the precision rifle is its limited ammunition. The Sniper receives only a limited number of bullets for each mission. Some missions allow him only three! Use your ammunition wisely.

TIP

After the Sniper fires the rifle, he stands up. Often he may be visible to the enemy. Therefore, try always to fire from a prone position. After taking the shot, quickly press [C] to drop prone. If you must shoot again, press [R] to bring the rifle back up.

PISTOL

The sniper, too, carries the Smith and Wesson W9 9mm pistol. However, he's usually too far from the action to use it.

FIRST AID KIT

When the Driver and Spy aren't assigned to a mission, the Sniper will act as the team's medic. Press [K] to open the first aid kit. The cursor will change to a syringe. Place it over a wounded Commando and click to restore some of his health. The first aid kit contains a limited number of doses, so use it only when absolutely necessary.

TIP

You'll rarely use the first aid kit. When your men are shot at, they usually die. If a Commando is wounded, it's because you made a mistake. Learn from it. Also, if you're near the end of a mission, use any remaining treatments on wounded Commandos to bring them back to full health. This will give you more points for the mission total.

TUTORIAL

The Sniper begins in the southwest corner. He must take out the six guards carefully. You have only six bullets, so make them count. Soldier 1 patrols near your start position. Put your Sniper into a crawl (C). When Soldier 1 heads away from you, quickly crawl east toward the tree near the flag. Every time the Sniper fires, he'll stand. Therefore, in a situation where other enemies may see you, press C to have the Sniper quickly drop prone after firing. Now bring up the precision rifle (R). Target Soldier 1. You want to kill him out of sight of other guards. Wait until he nears the rock; then click to fire. Drop prone immediately and target Soldier 2. When he's at the southern end of his route, fire again and drop prone. Kill Soldier 3 when he's near the corner of the fence.

Crawl west a bit so you can target Soldier 4 when he nears the door of the mock building. Place the crosshairs near the door and fire when 4 walks into the center. Stand up and run toward the northeast corner. Shift-click on Soldier 5 to see what he sees. Before you come into his line of sight, drop prone and crawl the rest of the

Figure 2-2. Six soldiers patrol the area. It's a good thing the Sniper has six bullets. Remember—one shot, one kill.

way. Bring up the rifle and shoot 5. Soldier 6 will see the body and run to take a look. Take him out, as well, with your last bullet. Then make your way to the flag to end the training session. Nice shooting!

THE MARINE

The Marine is another silent killer. Instead of hiding in a hole like the Green Beret, he can hide underwater and pop up to kill unsuspecting enemies. The Marine is available in most missions, except for those in North Africa (for obvious reasons). His ability to move undetected underwater means you can send him behind enemy lines to attack from a different angle from the rest of your Commando team.

VITAL STATISTICS

Name: James Blackwood, a.k.a. "Fins"

Date of Birth: August 11, 1911

Place of Birth: Melbourne

Country: Australia

Rank: Soldier

Height: 6 ft. 1 in.

Weight: 181 lbs.

BACKGROUND

1935: Enlists in the Royal Navy

1936: Promoted to captain

1938: Demoted to sergeant after an "incident" during a stopover in Hawaii

1940: Due to further conduct problems, the General Staff gives him a choice of expulsion from the armed forces or joining the Commandos as an ordinary soldier.

MILITARY RECORD

DUNKIRK

Receives the Military Cross for heroism after rescuing 45 soldiers who were surrounded on the beach and about to be captured.

ADDITIONAL INFO

Dissolute character, loves a good time

Great gambler

Problems with alcohol apparently under control

Naval Engineer, studied at Oxford

Member for three years of the rowing team that won the regatta between Oxford and Cambridge

Great swimmer; first to swim cross the English Channel (on a bet)

Sailing skills make him invaluable in missions involving naval operations

SKILLS AND EQUIPMENT

COMBAT KNIFE

The Marine carries the Wilkinson Sword combat knife, like the Green Beret, and he's just as skilled in using it.

SPEARGUN

Because there are no underwater enemies, the Marine uses the speargun much like a silenced gun. Its drawbacks are its short range and slow rate of fire. Reloading takes a few seconds between each shot. To bring up the spear gun, press [J].

The Marine uses the speargun effectively by swimming up to a target, popping out of the water, firing the speargun, and then dropping back into the water. He can take out a patrol one soldier at a time this way.

TIP

The Marine can single-handedly (and silently) take out a two-man patrol. While the soldiers are turned away from you, run after the rearmost soldier and kill him with the knife. Then quickly bring up the speargun and shoot the other enemy. To speed up your rate of fire, put the speargun away after every shot. Fire, right-click, press J, and fire again.

DIVING GEAR

Diving gear allows the Marine to travel underwater. When the Marine enters shallow water, diving gear appears in his knapsack. Press D to put it on and submerge. Press D when he's in shallow water to have him pop out. During a mission, always consider ways you might use the Marine's diving capability to your advantage.

If the Marine is spotted diving by the enemy, sometimes he will be shot at while underwater. Therefore, make sure he is out of enemy sight when submerging.

PISTOL

The Marine also carries the Smith and Wesson W9 9mm pistol. Use it when noise doesn't matter.

INFLATABLE BOAT

Although the Marine has no trouble crossing water, the other Commandos can't do so by themselves. However, they can ride across on the Marine's inflatable boat. Press B at the water's edge to pull it out of the knapsack. It inflates automatically when it hits the water. To climb in, move the cursor over the boat until it becomes a lever and click. The Marine will deflate the boat and put it back in his pack when you press H and click on the boat.

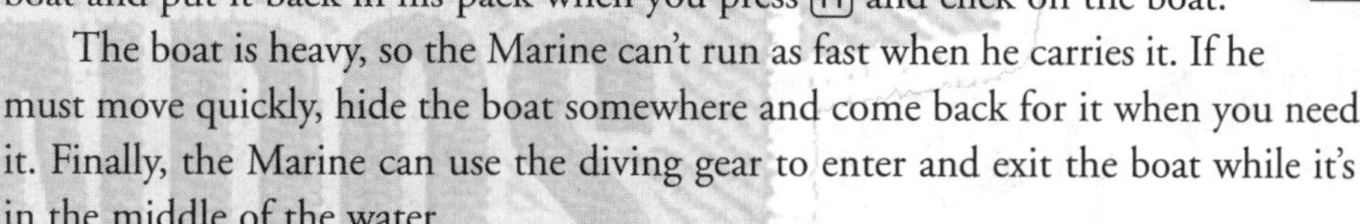

The boat is heavy, so the Marine can't run as fast when he carries it. If he must move quickly, hide the boat somewhere and come back for it when you need it. Finally, the Marine can use the diving gear to enter and exit the boat while it's in the middle of the water.

When deploying the boat, make sure you do it in shallow water. Inflating it close to the water will not work.

TUTORIAL

The Marine begins in the northeast. To get to the water, he must kill two soldiers right at the start. Move near Soldier 1 and pull out the knife (X). As 2 walks away, knife 1, and then run after 2. Place the cursor ahead of 2, along his path. Then, while running, press J to bring up the speargun and place the cursor over 2. When you're in range, the red circle-and-slash will disappear from the targeting cursor and you can click to fire. Now head for the water. When you're in shallow water, the diving gear appears in your knapsack. Put it on (D).

Swim to the steps near Soldier 3 until the diving gear reappears. Look around to make sure 4 and 5 can't see you; then pop out of the water by pressing D, bring up the speargun (J), fire at 3, lower the gun (right-click) and then move onto the steps until the diving gear appears. Put it on and re-enter the water. Stay by the steps. Soldiers 4 and 5 eventually will see the body and come to investigate one at a time. Kill each as you did 3.

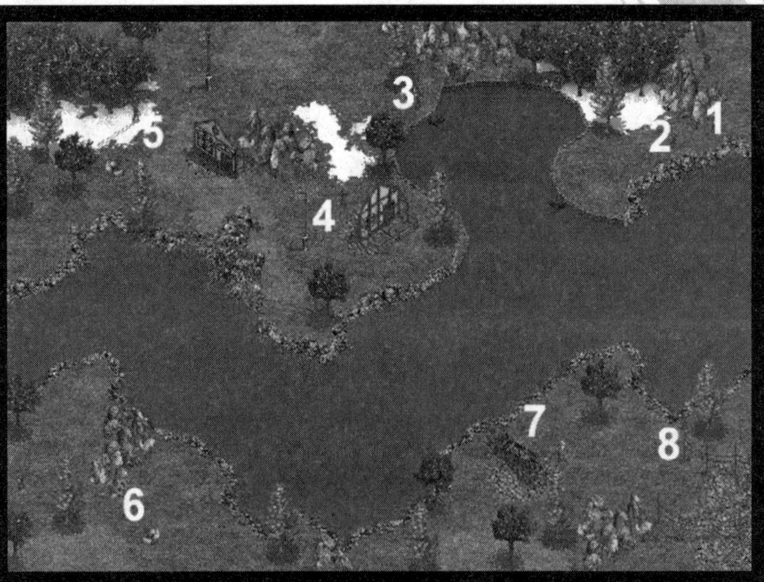

Figure 2-3. The Marine uses the water to move unseen around the map and easily can kill enemies wandering too close to shore.

This tactic of popping up out of the water, firing, and then jumping back in is particularly effective for taking out patrols of more than one soldier.

Now swim toward Soldier 6. He won't get close enough to the water to use the foregoing tactic, so position the Marine east of Soldier 6's route. When he turns and heads west, leave the water and run after him. Kill him with either the knife or the speargun—it's your choice.

Let's try out the boat. Walk over to the water and press [B] to bring out the boat. It will self-inflate in the water. To climb aboard, move the cursor over it until it turns into a hand and lever. The Marine is the only Commando who can operate water craft. Row out to the middle of the lake. Boats aren't as smart as Commandos: if you give a boat a destination, it moves toward it in a straight line. If it meets an obstacle, it just gets stuck, where a Commando will walk around.

The Marine can don his diving gear while he's in the boat. Put it on, swim around the boat, and then hop back in. Row to Soldier 7, landing east of him. To leave the boat, click on the picture of the Marine in the knapsack. Then press [H] to bring up the pick-up cursor, and click on the boat to put it back in your pack. While keeping an eye on Soldier 7's view, sneak up on him and kill him with the knife. Finally, walk over to 8 and shoot him in the back with the pistol ([G]). Why not? No one's around to hear. Walk over to the flag to end the session. Now put on some dry clothes.

THE SAPPER

Many missions require your Commandos to destroy objectives. The Sapper usually is the one to do it. But blowing things up isn't his only skill. He also can kill silently and provide access to fenced-off areas.

VITAL STATISTICS

Name: Russell Hancock, a.k.a. "Inferno"
Date of Birth: January 14, 1911
Place of Birth: Liverpool
Country: England
Rank: Soldier
Height: 6 ft.
Weight: 175 lbs.

BACKGROUND

1933: Joins Liverpool Fire Department

1934: Joins high-risk Explosives Department

1939: Joins the army

1940: Volunteers for Commandos

MILITARY RECORD

OPERATION CHARIOT

During the assault on St. Nazaire, he's responsible for explosions that caused many casualties in the German garrison and rendered port installations useless for many months. The Germans captured him during this operation. After two months, he escaped prison camp (on his fifth attempt) and returned to England.

ADDITIONAL INFO

Outstanding valor and daring, even rashness

Wide knowledge of explosives and extensive experience using explosions

Skilled in explosives manufacture from almost any material

SKILLS AND EQUIPMENT

TRAP

The Sapper carries a trap that can kill an enemy soldier without a sound. Think of this giant "bear trap" as a silent land mine. The Sapper places the trap when you press J. When an enemy soldier walks over it, he's killed instantly. To recover the trap, press H and click on the trap. Set the trap in an enemy's path or near a soldier. Lure him into the trap with the Green Beret's decoy, or with footprints in snow or sand. It's a lot of fun finding ways to lure enemies into the trap.

PISTOL

The Sapper also carries the Smith and Wesson W9 9mm pistol.

GRENADES

The Sapper is the only Commando who can handle grenades. He can throw these fragmentation grenades about the same distance a pistol can shoot, but grenades can go *over* obstacles. The resulting explosion takes out all enemies (or friends) within the blast radius. To use a grenade, press [E] and then click on the target. Grenades also can destroy tanks and other armored vehicles. Its explosion will attract attention, and could even set off an alarm, so use the grenade carefully, or when sound doesn't matter.

> **TIP**
>
> Grenades are great for taking out an entire patrol at once. When using one, try to kill as many soldiers as possible. For instance, wait until a patrol passes near another soldier and kill them all with a single grenade.

TIME BOMB

The time bomb consists of explosives detonated by a timer. To place the time bomb, move the Sapper to the target location and press [B]. You'll have approximately 10 seconds to get away before the bomb explodes. Although the time bomb will take out most structures and vehicles, it won't destroy concrete or fortified buildings.

REMOTE CONTROL BOMB

The remote control bomb gives the same results as the time bomb, but the Sapper can detonate it any time after placing it. Place the bomb with [B] and press [A] to detonate it. You can place more than one remote control bomb before detonating them. The first time you press [A], the first bomb you placed will detonate.

Pressing it again detonates the second bomb you placed, and so forth. The Sapper can detonate bombs from anywhere on the map. He needn't be within a certain radius of the bomb.

TIP

When placing a bomb, make sure you position it so it will destroy the target. If sand bags or concrete cover part of the target, place the bomb near the unprotected side; otherwise, the target may not be destroyed. If possible, place and detonate bombs for secondary damage, such as killing a passing patrol.

WIRE CUTTERS

In some missions, you must get past a wire fence. The Sapper can carry a pair of wire cutters that will get you through. But don't use them on an electric fence unless the power is off. Also, the cutters can't cut barbed wire.

TUTORIAL

Although the Sapper usually blows things up, he also can kill silently using the trap. He begins in the southwest. When Soldier 1 moves north, run to the wall and place the trap in his path (J). Then move quickly behind the rock, careful to not be seen by Soldier 2. Soldier 1 will walk into the trap and be killed. To retrieve the trap, press H and click on it.

Move toward the opening in the wall. When Soldier 3 heads away, sneak through, and then toward 2. Drop prone and crawl to the east side of the woods to stay out of view. When 2 heads away, stand (S), and run to place the trap in 2's path in the snow. Then run back to your hiding spot and drop prone. Soldier 2 will see your footprints and come after you, but the trap will stop him. Crawl over and retrieve the trap, as well as grenades from the crate near the parachute.

Figure 2-4.
The Sapper must kill all the guards, blow up the two mock buildings, and destroy the tank.

Next, crawl toward Soldier 3. Press [E] to bring out a grenade and throw it at 3. Crouch and hide, because Patrol 4 will hear the explosion and come running. Throw another grenade at the patrol to kill them all. Walk near each building and plant explosives by pressing [B]. Now take out the tank. Crawl toward it and hide by the large rock in the north. When the tank approaches, get close to its path and throw a grenade when it's in range.

Having eliminated the soldiers and tank, all that's left is to blow the buildings. Press [A] to set off the first explosive, and again to detonate the second. During this training session, you used remote control bombs. In some missions, you'll have time bombs that will explode about 10 seconds after you place them. Way to blow things up!

THE DRIVER

The Driver is probably the least used of all the Commandos. During multiplayer games, you do not want to be the Driver unless you like watching the others play. However, when it comes time to use him, it's usually a lot of fun. He's the only Commando who can operate vehicles.

VITAL STATISTICS

Name: Sid Perkins

Date of Birth: April 4, 1910

Place of Birth: Brooklyn

Country: USA

Rank: Soldier

Height: 6 ft. 2 in.

Weight: 183 lbs.

BACKGROUND

1934–37: Car mechanic by day, thief by night

1937: Leaves for England, fleeing a prison sentence

1938: Sought by American authorities, enlists in the British Army

1938–40: Collaborates with the Foreign Office in testing vehicles and arms stolen from the enemy

1941: Meets Paddy Maine, who recruits him for the Commandos

MILITARY RECORD

TAMET AIRFIELD

Together with the Long Range Desert Group (LRDG), after destroying eight German fighters with his jeep's machine gun and with no ammunition left, the Driver eliminated four more by smashing his vehicle into them. He suffered severe burns.

ORAN BEACH

Decorated for holding off a company of Italian regulars in a captured German tank, enabling the extraction of a squad of collaborators.

ADDITIONAL INFO

Mistrustful; relates poorly to teammates

Long criminal career in the USA (car theft, armed robbery, and so on)

Wide knowledge of mechanics; can drive and repair any land vehicle

During time in the Foreign Office, acquired skill in handling all types of arms

Loves to gamble and smoke cigars

Fluent in Spanish

SKILLS AND EQUIPMENT

PISTOL

The Sapper, too, carries the Smith and Wesson W9 9mm pistol.

MACHINE GUN

During some missions, the Driver may be assigned a machine gun or pick one up from an aerial drop. To pull out the machine gun, press [M]. The cursor will become a reticle. Click on a target to fire a burst. The machine gun isn't silent and will attract attention, but a single burst can take out an entire patrol. It never runs out of ammunition.

FIRST AID KIT

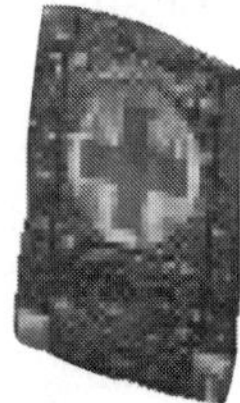

The Driver is the team medic and carries the first aid kit. (If he's not in the mission, the Spy or the Sniper act as medic.) Press [K] to open the first aid kit; then click on a wounded Commando to restore some of his health.

VEHICLES

The Driver is the only Commando who can drive land vehicles. Place the cursor over an unoccupied vehicle until it becomes a lever; then click to enter. Vehicles can carry other team members, but only the Driver can operate them.

To drive, move the cursor to a destination and click. The vehicle will move to

the destination in a straight line. If it encounters an obstacle, it will run into it and stop. Therefore, you must steer the vehicle by giving it a series of waypoints. Some vehicles, such as tanks and half-tracks, are armed. The Driver can fire at enemies by Ctrl-clicking. You also can run over soldiers by driving fast when you hit them. To drive fast, double-click on the destination.

GUN POSITIONS

The Driver also can take control of unoccupied gun positions, such as machine guns nests or artillery posts. Place the cursor over the gun until it becomes a lever and then click to take control. The cursor will become a targeting reticle. Just place it over a target and click to fire.

TUTORIAL

The Driver begins in the southwest. Notice that he's armed only with a pistol. When Soldier 1 walks away, run out behind him, bring up the pistol (G), and shoot three times to kill him. Soldier 2 will hear the shots and come to investigate. Right-click to lower the gun and run behind a rock. When Soldier 2 turns to leave, run out and shoot him, as well.

One of the soldiers may have shot you. Even though you take no damage in training, let's practice using the first aid kit. Press K; the cursor becomes a syringe. Click on the Driver (or, during the missions, another Commando) to administer healing.

Next, crawl around the wall toward the air-dropped crate, where you can pick up a machine gun. Approach Soldier 3 from the south and pull out the machine gun (M). Soldiers 4 and 5 probably won't react. If they do, drop prone and let *them* have it with the machine gun, as well. Otherwise, walk up behind them and hose them down with hot lead. With no one guarding the tank, place the cursor over it until it becomes a hand-and-lever and click to hop in. To drive the tank, click in the direction you want to move in and establish waypoints. Double-click to drive fast. A fast-moving vehicle can run over enemy troops and kill them. A slow vehicle will only push them out of the way. If the vehicle, such as a tank, has a form of armament, Ctrl-click will fire the weapon—in this case, the machine gun. Drive the tank east,

Figure 2-5.
The Driver will use firearms for killing all the soldiers in this training session, because he has no way to kill silently.

taking out Patrol 6 with the tank's machine guns. Finally, steer over to the flag to end the training session. Good driving!

THE SPY

Although you'll get the Spy in only nine of your 20 missions, you can use him more—and definitely need him for those nine. The Spy can wear disguises and walk among the enemy. He's also a very serious silent killer.

VITAL STATISTICS

Name: Rene Duchamp, a.k.a. "Spooky"

Date of Birth: November 20, 1911

Place of Birth: Lyons

Country: France

Rank: Soldier

Height: 6 ft. 4 in.

Weight: 179 lbs.

BACKGROUND

1934: Joins French Secret Service

1935–38: Chief of Security at the French Embassy in Berlin

1939: Enlists in the French Army

1940: After the German invasion, joins the Resistance; he collaborates occasionally with the British Commandos in special operations

MILITARY RECORD

The Spy has participated in a number of sabotages, and is responsible for destroying at least three trains, 14 tanks, and more than 30 land vehicles. His information about the position and movement of the German troops is invaluable to the British Secret Service.

He infiltrated the Italian Command Center and eliminated the commander of the Turin Garrison, stole the defensive layout of the Anzio region, and evaded capture for two days.

ADDITIONAL INFO

Amiable character, great conversationalist

Feels absolute hatred for the Germans

Time in the Secret Service made him expert in communications, infiltration, and sabotage

Speaks French, German, English, Italian, and Russian fluently

SKILLS AND EQUIPMENT

SYRINGE WITH POISON

The Spy carries a syringe and a bottle of poison. He pulls it out when you press [L]. The cursor will become a syringe. Place it over the target and click to administer a lethal injection. The enemy will die immediately and silently.

PISTOL

The Spy carries a standard-issue Smith and Wesson W9 9mm pistol.

GERMAN UNIFORM

The Spy can walk among the enemy only when he wears an SS general's uniform. He begins some missions equipped with such a uniform; in others, he must acquire one from a clothesline. In those cases, place the cursor over the clothesline until it becomes a lever. Click and the Spy will walk to the clothesline and don the uniform. He'll maintain his disguise until he's spotted killing or carrying a body. To put the disguise on again after losing it, move out of the enemy's sight and press [U].

FIRST AID KIT

When the Driver is absent from a mission, the Spy fulfills the role of medic. He administers first aid when you press [K] and then click on a wounded Commando.

DISTRACT

One of the Spy's most useful skills is his ability to distract enemy soldiers. With his fluent German, he can carry on a conversation and keep the enemy's view locked in one direction for as long as you want. This allows other Commandos to sneak past a guard or kill enemy soldiers undetected. To distract enemies, approach from the direction toward which you want them to look and press [D] to change the cursor to an officer's hat. Then click on the enemy you wish to distract. When distracted soldiers hear gunfire, explosions, or an alarm, they immediately return to duty.

CARRY BODIES

Like the Green Beret, the Spy can carry bodies. This is useful for removing the poisoned corpses before enemy soldiers spot them.

TUTORIAL

The Spy begins the session in the west. Watch Soldier 4 as he walks his route. When he turns and heads away from Soldier 1, pull out the syringe of poison (L) and click on Soldier 1. He'll die instantly and silently. Right-click to put the poison away. Press H to pick up the body; then move it toward the rock. Drop it by right-clicking.

Soldier 2 is your next target. When he reaches the southern limit of his walk and turns around, run after him and give him a lethal injection, as well. Do the same with Soldier 3.

Now you must get the German uniform from the clothesline. Wait until Soldier 5 walks west and 6 begins to look west. Place the cursor over the uniform. When the cursor turns into a lever, double-click to run quickly to the uniform and put it on. By the time 6 looks at the clothesline, he'll see a German officer.

Figure 2-6. The Spy, in his German officer's uniform, can walk among the enemy and even talk to them.

Walk over near the building where Soldier 4 is patrolling. When he turns around, kill him with the pistol. If he looks at you, you'll lose your disguise. Press [U] to put it on again before the other guards can see you. They'll come to see what happened, but they won't suspect you. After all, you're one of them. Eventually they'll return to their posts. Walk to one of the soldiers and strike up a conversation using the Distract command (press [D] and click on the target). The attention of the soldier you're distracting will lock on you. (To have a soldier look in the opposite direction, approach from behind.) Poison Soldier 5 when he begins walking east. Finally, kill Soldier 6 any way you want and walk to the flag to end the training. *Sehr gut!**

*German for "very good"—but the Spy should know that.

CHAPTER 3

ADVANCED SCHOOL

Now that you're proficient with game basics and skilled at controlling your Commandos, it's time to discuss strategy and tactics. Strategy is the overall plan for completing a mission—determining what you must do to achieve the objective. Tactics are the steps your Commandos take to accomplish the goals, such as how you'll kill a certain soldier or how you'll sneak into an enemy base. You must first form a strategy for a mission, and then choose tactics for making the strategy a success.

TIP

Because the missions are timed for points, it's a good idea to save the mission right at the start. Determine your strategy. Then, when you're ready, restart the mission at the beginning. The time you take working on your strategy won't accrue to your mission time.

FORMING A STRATEGY

Each of *COMMANDOS*' missions requires you to form a strategy before issuing orders to your men. You could probably survive the first few without planning ahead, but not so in later missions.

How do you create a strategy? The planning breaks down into four parts—objective, requirements for achieving the objective, implementation, and flexibility. Throughout this chapter we'll use "Baptism of Fire" as the example for each.

Planning a trip is a good analogy for planning your mission. First, you decide where to go—your objective. Next, you determine how you'll reach your destination—transportation, route, what to take along, and so forth. Then you depart—implement your plan. However, if something in your plan fails, you must cope with the unexpected—that is, you must be flexible. For example, if the car breaks down

Figure 3-1.
Printing a copy of the mission map makes planning strategy easier. Mark the locations and routes of the enemy soldiers using colored pens.

TIP

In *COMMANDOS* it's a good idea to print out a copy of the mission map, locate all the enemy soldiers on it, and mark their locations and routes (if moving). This gives you a hard copy to look at before and during the mission. To make a map, press Print Screen and print from within a graphics program.

or you lose your luggage, you must change your plans accordingly, so you can still reach your destination and do what you planned when you get there.

OBJECTIVE

The most important part of planning a strategy is determining your objectives. Many a battle has been lost by a failure to identify quantifiable objectives. In all of your missions, you will receive your objective during the pre-mission briefing. Look over the written orders during the game. Sometimes further objectives show up *after* the briefing. For example, your mission may be to assassinate a German general officer. However, by the time you begin the mission, Command also may have ordered you to destroy enemy headquarters while you're in the area. Always check your objectives both before and during a mission. Just think of how frustrating it would be to complete a mission, with all the hard work that entails, only to realize you can't go on to the next mission because you failed to achieve an objective left unmentioned during the pre-mission briefing!

Zoom out the map and locate your objectives. Take time to look over the opposition. In the first mission, your objective is to blow up the relay station. You'll see that water separates your Commandos from the objective. Keeping all this in mind, go on to the next stage of planning.

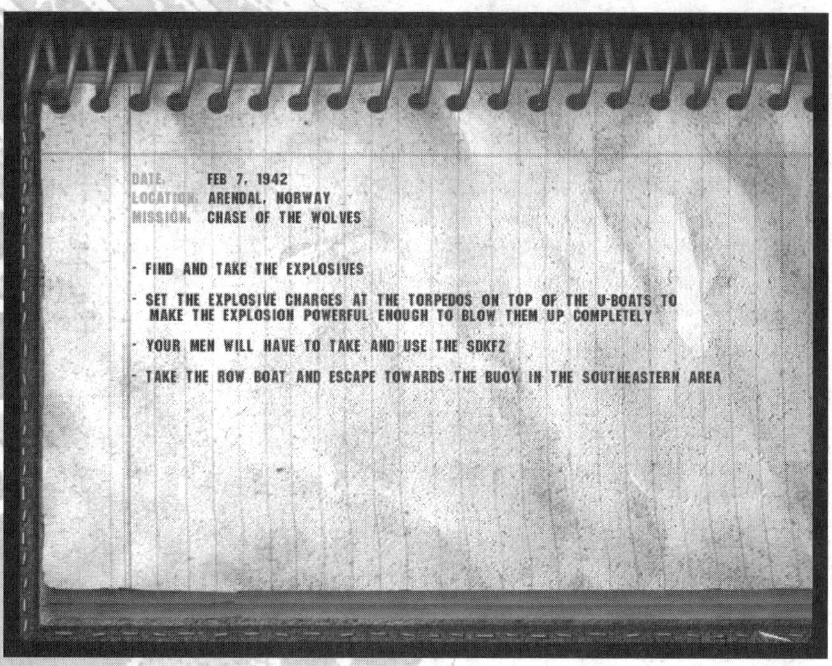

DATE: FEB 7, 1942
LOCATION: ARENDAL, NORWAY
MISSION: CHASE OF THE WOLVES
- FIND AND TAKE THE EXPLOSIVES
- SET THE EXPLOSIVE CHARGES AT THE TORPEDOS ON TOP OF THE U-BOATS TO MAKE THE EXPLOSION POWERFUL ENOUGH TO BLOW THEM UP COMPLETELY
- YOUR MEN WILL HAVE TO TAKE AND USE THE SDKFZ
- TAKE THE ROW BOAT AND ESCAPE TOWARDS THE BUOY IN THE SOUTHEASTERN AREA

Figure 3-2.
Check the map. Check your printed orders during the mission, as well. Objectives may have been added since the pre-mission briefing. You might also find a few hints on how to succeed.

PHASES

After determining your objectives, you must form a plan for achieving them. First, decide how you can accomplish the objective. Many missions require you to destroy a building or installation. How will it be destroyed? What equipment will you use? Do you have the equipment you need? If not, how can you get it? In the Mission 1 example, none of your men carry explosives, so they must find another way to blow up the relay station. As you look around, you notice several explosive barrels on the island with the target. The Green Beret can move these next to the relay station and shoot them to destroy it.

You must determine what steps to take in order to achieve your objective. How will your men reach the objective area? What paths or transportation will they use? This is the first, "maneuver," phase.

Next, if they need additional equipment, locate it and determine how you'll acquire it. For instance, if you need explosives, are they available to steal from the enemy? Or have your allies dropped supplies by parachute somewhere on the map?

The third phase is taking care of business once you reach the objective. Once you accomplish that, you must get your men to safety. Escape is the final phase.

In the Mission 1 example, we solved the equipment problem: the Commandos will use the barrels on the relay station island. This tells you you must get the Green Beret, the only one who can lift barrels, to the northern island. However, he's separated from the objective by water. There's a boat on the island with the Marine. The boat is the equipment necessary to transport the Green Beret to the objective island. Then, as part of your planning, you must figure out how to get the Green Beret and boat together. The Marine must kill all the soldiers on his island to get to the boat; the Green Beret, with the help of the Driver, must eliminate all soldiers on *their* island so they can get to the dock. Then you must row all Commandos across the water. For the Green Beret to move the barrels safely, you must deal with the enemy guards. With the coast clear, you can destroy the rely station. For this mission, you don't need an escape, so you can skip this phase.

Figure 3-3. When your Commandos begin a mission lacking some vital equipment, they must get it from air drops or steal it from the enemy.

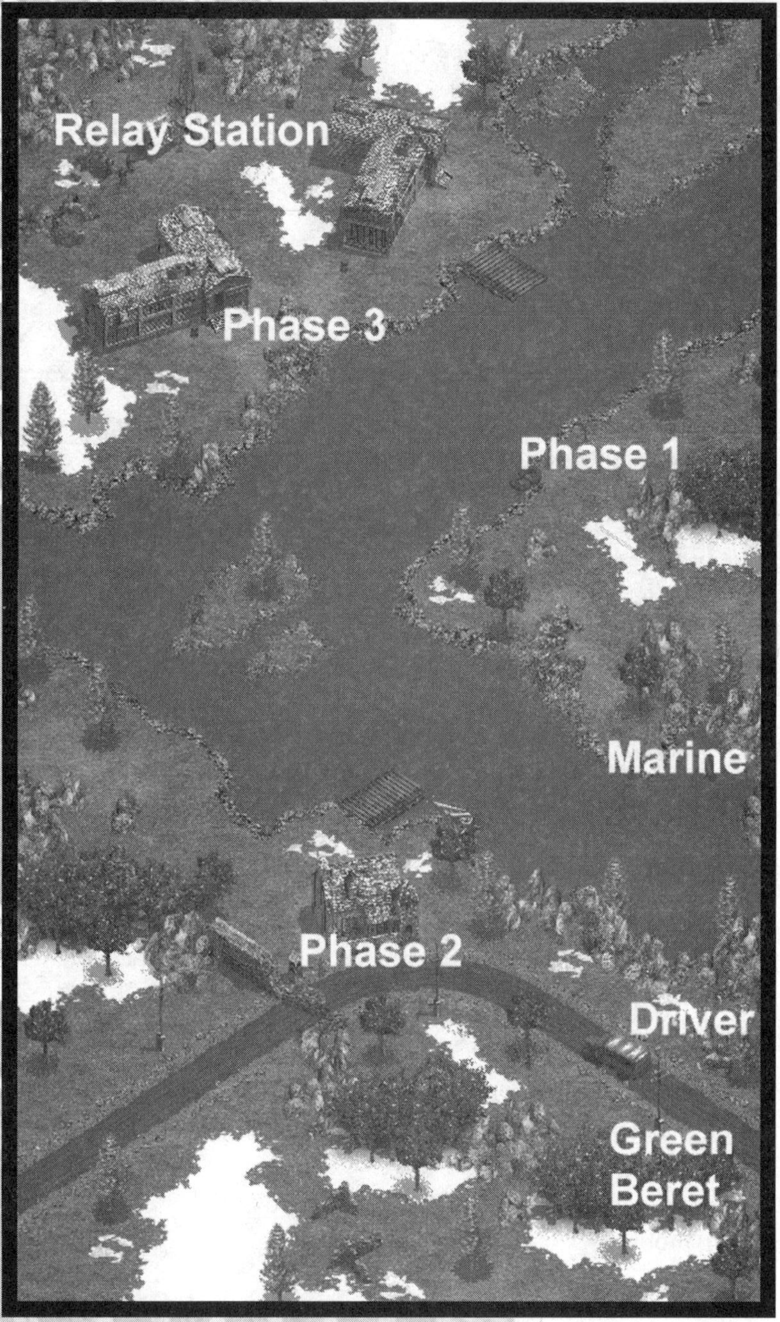

Figure 3-4.
Mission 1 breaks down into three phases.

Almost every mission has four main phases—equipment, maneuver, execution, and escape. More complex missions may require more than four phases, because you may have to maneuver to the equipment, maneuver to an objective, maneuver to another objective, and finally maneuver to your means of escape.

TIP

For some missions, it's easier to plan your strategy in reverse. For example, find a way of escape, and then figure out how to get there from the objective. Continue backward from the objective to the equipment, and then from the equipment to the Commandos' start position. As you're setting up your route, look and see what opposition you'll face along the way and try to find the path of least resistance.

IMPLEMENTATION

Now that you've divided your mission into phases, it's time to implement them. This is where you put your strategy into practice, using tactics to complete each phase.

FLEXIBILITY

In war, a plan rarely survives the first shot intact. Therefore, it behooves a good commander to be flexible. If you can't complete one of your phases for some reason, modify your strategy to reach its goal. No matter how good your initial strategy, you'll probably have to make minor adjustments to factors you hadn't considered would begin causing problems.

TACTICS FOR SUCCESS

Tactics fit under the "implementation" strategy area. A phase may call for you to clear an area of enemy soldiers; you'll use tactics during the mission to carry out the orders for the phase.

In a way, *COMMANDOS* is like a puzzle game: you must determine an order in which to eliminate enemies. These "kill orders" make up a big part of tactics. You also can break tactics down into parts. You'll use all of this to achieve your goals for a phase. Completed phases in turn lead to a successful mission, and advancement to the next mission. Now let's take a look at some good tactics to learn and use.

PATIENCE

Although you receive points for completing a mission quickly, *COMMANDOS* does not reward rushing into things. At the start of each phase, study the enemies in the area. Observe not only their locations and patrol routes, but also what they can see. In many missions, enemies are positioned to keep an eye on one another. Watch their actions to find the weak link in their defense, such as which soldier you can kill first; this allows you to kill a second soldier, and so on. If time is a concern, save the

Figure 3-5.
Check out what enemy soldiers can and can't see before rushing in to kill.

mission at the beginning of a phase. Then, after studying the enemy, restart the mission at your save and continue, with no penalty for your planning time.

The other reason patience is important is timing. Many times you must wait to kill a soldier until another soldier or soldiers look or walk away from you. When multiple soldiers are involved, you may have to wait for them to make several rounds before all enemies are looking away from your target at the same time.

STEALTH

You command a team of two to six men, *not* an armored division. Therefore, your team can't go barreling in with guns blazing. Stealth and surprise are your greatest allies. If you think there are a lot of enemy soldiers, just wait until an alarm sounds and reinforcements pour out of the barracks. The key to success is to stay hidden, out of sight, and operate silently. As we pointed out in Chapter 1, your enemies can not only see, but can hear and yell out warnings and alarms, as well. You want to

Figure 3-6. The Sapper's trap kills silently. However, you must position it so other enemy soldiers won't see the body.

move across the map unobserved. Many times, enemy soldiers present obstacles to your movement. Then you must kill them unnoticed before you can continue.

Killing silently isn't always enough. A dead soldier is a dead body: if other enemy soldiers see it, they'll come to investigate and may catch you. They may also sound an alarm and ruin your advantage of surprise. If there are other soldiers in the area, you must either kill enemies where their bodies will fall unseen or physically hide the bodies afterward. Because only the Green Beret and the Spy can move bodies, the other Commandos must kill with care.

KILLING THE ENEMY

No matter how carefully you crawl around the map, you'll have to kill enemy soldiers to reach your objectives. This is war, and war isn't pretty. However, you're seriously—and literally—outgunned. A shooting match easily can leave your men the losers. Enemy rifles and machine guns can kill a lot quicker than your pistol. Besides, gunfire makes noise, alerting other enemy soldiers to your presence, and before long you'll be outgunned *and* outnumbered. Therefore, kill silently. Don't let the target know what's happening until it's too late. Not every Commando can kill silently: only a few weapons are quiet. These include the knife, trap, speargun,

Figure 3-7.
The Green Beret is an expert at killing silently with the knife. He also can move the body out of sight afterward.

precision rifle, and syringe of poison. Silence is supreme, and these will become your weapons of choice.

However, there are times when you must use a noisy weapon, such as a pistol, machine gun, or grenades. Doing so is fine if no one except the target will hear, or if you're prepared for the enemy to come looking. You can kill soldiers as a result of another action, as well. For example, if you plant explosives near an objective, try to position them and time the explosion to kill a passing patrol or soldier. You also may want to use the sound to cause a reaction.

DECEPTION

Deception is a great tool for getting out of tight spots. There are two main ways to deceive the enemy. The first is to distract their attention. The Spy can do this when he wears the German officer's uniform. Using the Distract command, he walks up

Figure 3-8.
The Spy, once in uniform, can distract an entire enemy patrol with his great conversational ability and fluent German.

to an enemy soldier or patrol and addresses them, focusing their attention in one direction. The Green Beret's decoy can do the same. The Spy can distract until something else, such as a gunshot or alarm, attracts the enemy's attention, but the decoy works for only a limited time. After the enemy loses interest in it, they'll usually sound an alarm instead of just walking back to their post. Distraction allows other Commandos to sneak past the enemy or perform other actions unseen by the distracted party.

Another form of deception is luring soldiers away from their posts to kill them out of sight of other enemies. The decoy is good for this, as are footprints in snow or sand. When the enemy sees footprints, they go to investigate and either walk into the Sapper's trap or into an ambush. If neither sand nor snow are present, you can have a Commando briefly move into an enemy's field of view. Leaving a soldier's body where he died or moving the body into an enemy's view also works.

The Green Beret is the master of deception. Not only does he use the decoy effectively, but he also can dig himself into sand or snow to hide from the enemy. The Spy also is skilled at camouflage, but in a different way: his fluency in foreign languages and his stolen uniform allow him to walk among the enemy unnoticed.

Figure 3-9. The Green Beret leaves footprints in the snow to lure a soldier around the corner.

TEAMWORK

I often refer to your group of Commandos as a team. This is not a hastily chosen term. Your Commandos, with their individually unique skills and abilities, must work together as a team to carry out their missions. In our example from Mission 1, all three Commandos must work together. Only the Green Beret can lift the barrels and carry them to the relay station. But he can't cross the water alone. The Marine must provide a boat and row him to the island.

Often two Commandos must work together to kill a single soldier. For example, the Spy may distract a soldier while the Green Beret sneaks up to knife the unsuspecting enemy. The Green Beret also can use his decoy to lure an enemy soldier into a trap the Sapper sets. Notice that there are no missions with only one Commando. This is because each mission requires skills and abilities not available in a single man. During multiplayer games, there are no missions pitting one player against another. Instead, players must work together and communicate to complete each mission.

CHAPTER 4

THE NORWEGIAN CAMPAIGN

You must complete each of *COMMANDOS'* 20 linked missions before you can move on to the next. And "complete" means not only achieving your objective, but also keeping all your Commandos alive. If just one dies, you fail and must play the mission again.

In this chapter we provide strategy and tactics for completing the first seven missions—the Norwegian Campaign. Chapters 5 and 6 cover North African and European campaigns, respectively. The walkthrough format makes it easy for you to play with the book open nearby, and we go through each mission in steps, or "phases." Often in *COMMANDOS* you must perform tasks in sequence to reach an objective. And often you must finish one phase before moving to the next. Because some missions have many phases, it's a good idea to save your game as you complete each phase so you won't have to return to the mission's start if one of your Commandos dies.

Norway was one of the first areas where the newly formed Commandos were tested successfully. Most missions in the Norwegian campaign feature snow, and so your Commandos will leave footprints wherever they walk. If German guards spot these, they may follow. This can be a bad thing, but you can also use it to your advantage, luring enemies into traps and ambushes. The Green Beret can dig into and hide himself in the snow. A good commander will use this knowledge to give his or her Commandos an edge.

TIP

Most missions have several phases. Remember to save your game after completing each phase. That way, if a Commando dies, you need return only to the beginning of the phase, not the mission.

MISSION 1: BAPTISM OF FIRE

NORWAY, FEBRUARY 20, 1941

Since its retreat from Narvik in June 1940, Norway has remained under German occupation. The Luftwaffe has established important airfields at Trondheim, Herdla, and Stavanger, putting the whole North Sea in range of German bombers.

Your unit's first mission is to attack a poorly defended relay station at Sola as part of the incursion near the Stavanger airfield. This will block radio communications for some hours, delaying German reinforcements.

MISSION SUMMARY

Objective: Blow up the relay station on the northwestern island.

Team: Green Beret, Marine, Driver

Your team begins in the southern part of the map, separated from one another. You must obtain a boat to transport all your Commandos to the northwestern island. Several German soldiers and a machine-gun nest guard the relay station there.

PHASE 1: CAPTURE THE BOAT

To reach its objective, your team must cross the river. Because it has no boat, it must acquire one from the enemy. The boat is located on the island in the east, where your Marine begins the mission. Three enemy soldiers patrol the area, with one right next to the boat. Your Marine must eliminate them all as quietly as possible.

The Marine starts on the island's south shore. Have him move into the water immediately, don the diving gear, and swim to the north part of the island. Position him near the eastern map edge, close enough to land that he can get out of the water. Wait for Soldier 1 to walk past your man; then pop him up by pressing [D]. Immediately bring up the speargun (press [J]) and take the soldier out silently. Kill this enemy as close to the map edge as possible to keep the other enemy soldiers from discovering the body.

Return to the water and swim south, to where the Marine first got wet. Hide behind the rock there until Soldier 2 passes and heads back west. Run after him and take him out with either the speargun or the knife. Soldier 3 will continue

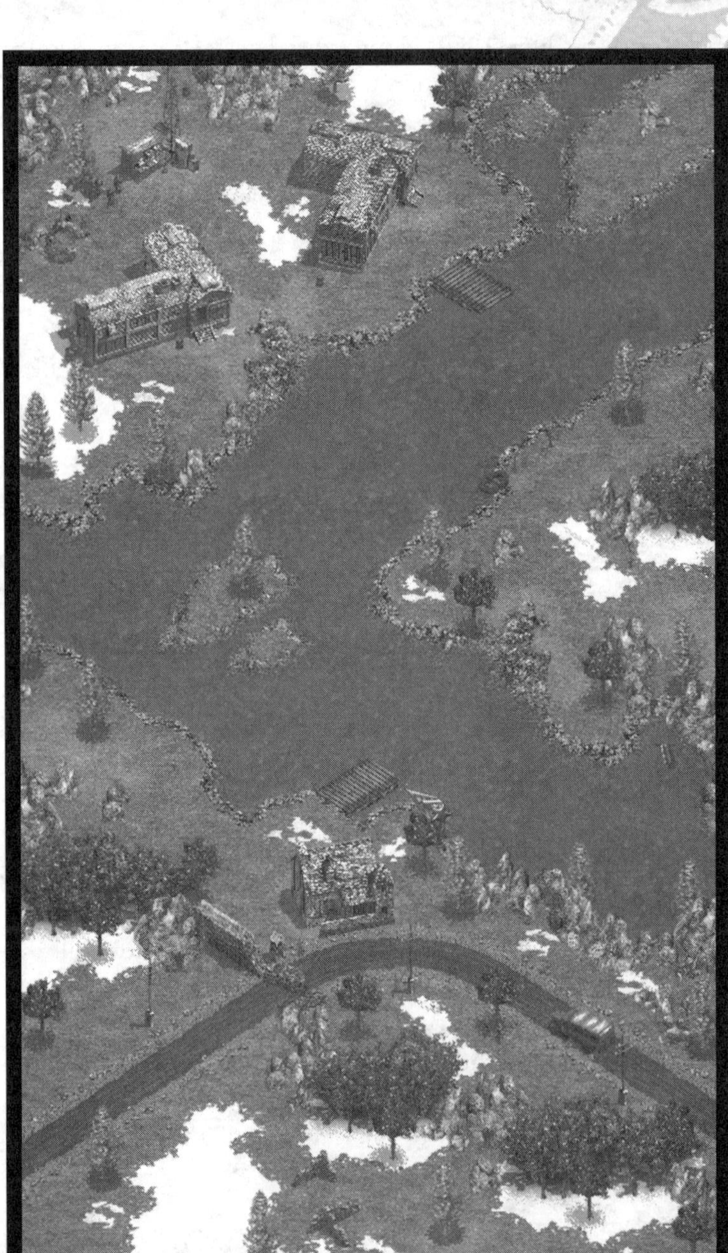

Figure 4-1.
Baptism of Fire

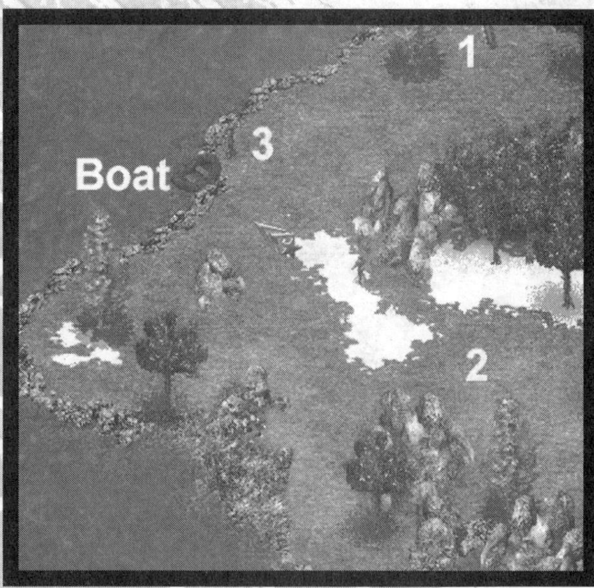

Figure 4-2.
The Marine must kill all three guards.

facing away from the action as long as you keep things quiet. Dispatch him with the speargun or knife, as well, and the boat is yours. Instead of boarding it and rowing, deflate it and store it in your pack by pressing [H] and selecting the boat.

Next, send the Marine to the north-central map area. There he'll find a couple of soldiers on patrol. Go for Soldier 4 first by swimming to a point west of his patrol and popping up, when he turns around, to take him out with the speargun. Then turn around and do the same for Soldier 5.

Finally, have the Marine swim to the southern island, to a point near the dock. For now, just keep him in the water. Save your game here.

PHASE 2: GET THE REST OF THE TEAM TO THE BOAT

Both the Green Beret and the Driver begin on the southern island, but they're separated. Four German soldiers block their way to the boat. The two Commandos must work together to get through.

The Green Beret should make the first move by running west and hiding behind the rubble. Watch Soldier 6 for a bit. When he turns and begins walking away, run and kill him with the knife by pressing [X].

Before you continue, shift-click on either Soldier 8 or Soldier 9 to see what they see. When they head back down toward the truck, run to the concrete wall and hide in the shadows. During their next trip down to the truck, climb the wall

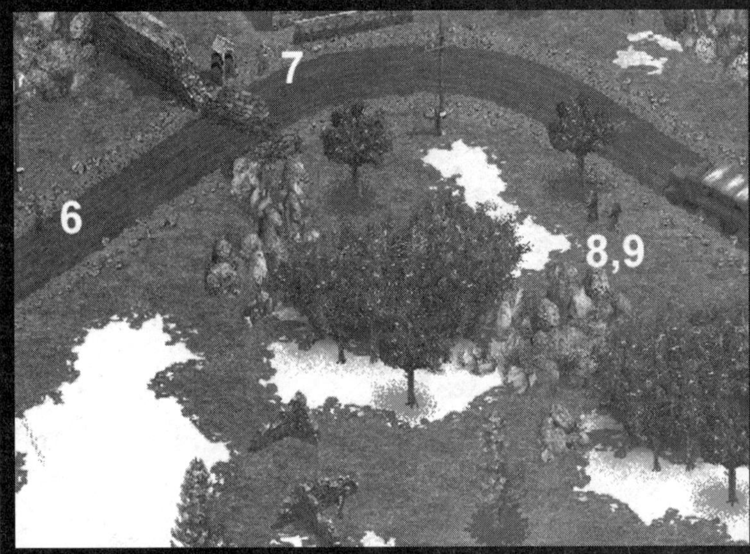

Figure 4-3. The Green Beret and Driver must kill all four soldiers on this island.

by moving the cursor onto it (the cursor becomes a pick). Descend the other side of the wall and run to the north side of the building to conceal the Green Beret from patrolling guards. Again, wait until they come close to the building and turn. Quickly run to Soldier 7, kill him with the knife, pick up the body by pressing H, and carry it behind the building, where you can dump it out of sight with a right-click.

Now you must take out the remaining two soldiers. You could do it by sending the Green Beret with the Marine to gun them down, but that can be risky. So try something clever: By now you're used to waiting for the guards to head south. When they do again, send the Green Beret out along the road, drop off the decoy, and then run back behind the building. As the enemy comes near the decoy, activate it. The two soldiers will walk over to the device and stare at it for a while.

Remember the Driver? It's time for some action on his part: Order him to climb into the truck. He'll start it automatically. Next, get the truck moving at high speed by double-clicking on the far side of the enemy. When the truck hits them, it kills both guards instantly. If you single-click, the truck will move slowly and won't kill

Figure 4-4.
The Driver runs over the unsuspecting guards with the truck while the decoy distracts them.

the Germans. Instead, they'll turn and shoot at the Driver, often killing him—and losing the mission for you.

Now that the area is secure, the Driver can climb out of the truck and head to the dock with the Green Beret. The Marine should surface and inflate the boat. When everybody's aboard, select the Marine (he's the only one who can row the boat) and head north.

PHASE 3: DESTROY THE RELAY STATION

Land on the south side of the northern island, behind the main building. Quickly move all your Commandos close to the building before the enemy spots them. There are a couple of ways to take out the three guards (10, 11, and 12) patrolling the relay station. Both involve the Green Beret:

Watch the patrolling guards and wait for them to begin moving north. Then order your Green Beret quickly to place either the decoy or a fuel barrel along their path, just east of the building; then run your man back behind the building. If you chose the fuel barrel, position the Green Beret as far south of the barrel as possible, while still in pistol range. As the guards approach the barrel, fire at it. They'll all go up in smoke.

If you use the decoy, activate it as they approach, and then send the Marine and Driver toward the machine-gun nest (13). After the Marine dispatches the

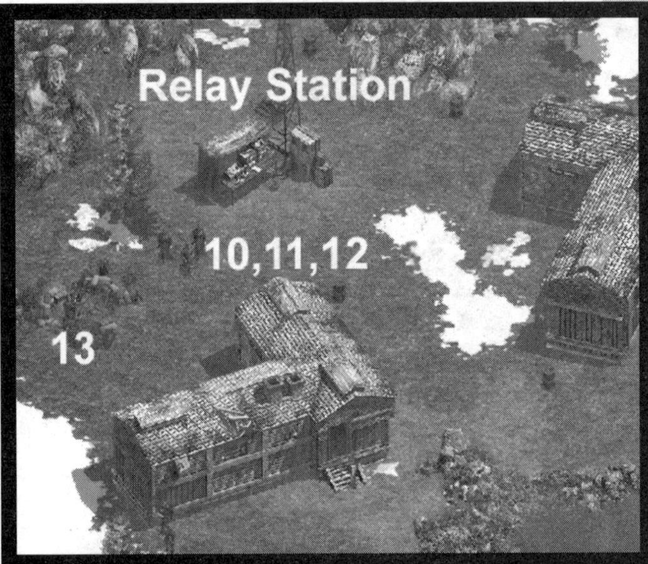

Figure 4-5.
The northern island contains several guards and a machine-gun nest.

Figure 4-6.
The Driver commandeers the machine gun and pours hot lead into the distracted patrol.

enemy soldier with the speargun, the Driver can fire the machine gun at the mesmerized German patrol.

Now that all the Germans are dead, the Green Beret must move a fuel barrel next to the relay station. Shoot at it with your choice of weapon to complete the mission.

MISSION 2: A QUIET BLOW-UP

NORWAY, MARCH 1, 1941

Operation Claymore, the first medium-scale incursion over Norway, has been approved. The objective is to neutralize industrial facilities and merchant ships in the Lofoten Islands, recruit Norwegian volunteers, and capture followers of collaborator Vidkun Quisling.

Your men will land in the Stamsund area, infiltrate a heavily defended camp near Storfjord while evading surveillance machine-gun nests and patrols, and blow up the fuel depot. This will shorten the range of enemy armored divisions for some days.

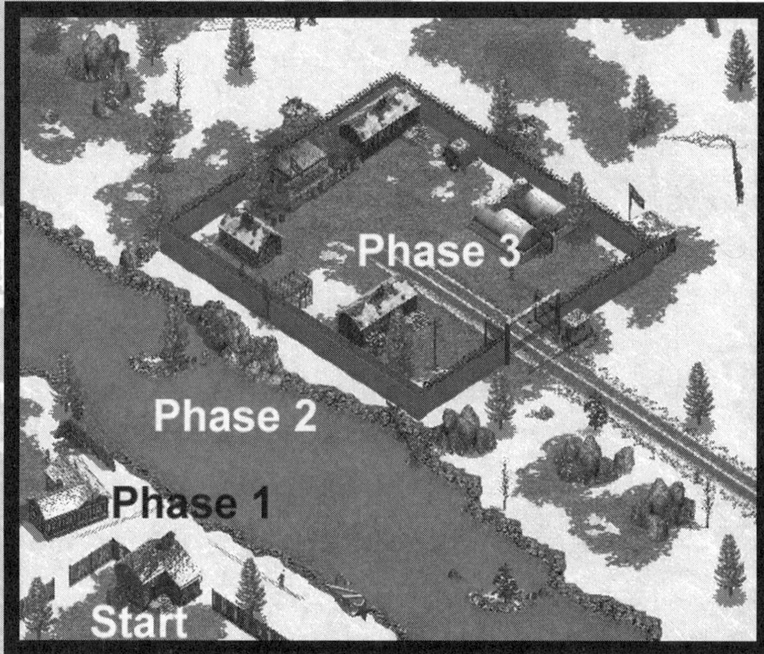

Figure 4-7.
A Quiet Blow-Up

MISSION SUMMARY

Objective: Blow up the fuel depot within the walled camp.

Team: Green Beret, Sniper, Marine, Sapper, Driver

This mission is a little tougher than the first. Remember, secrecy is the key. If a guard sounds the alarm, you'll have an extremely difficult time achieving your objective. The Commandos begin in the map's southwest corner. They must clear this area first and then make their way across the river. Beware! An enemy patrol boat motors up and down the river with a dual machine-gun mount that will seriously damage any Commando caught in its sights. Once across, you must make your way into the camp, plant the explosives near the fuel depot, and then make your escape in a commandeered truck.

PHASE 1: CLEAR THE WEST SHORE

The first phase can be difficult. You must eliminate all three enemy soldiers in this area before you can cross the river. Their routes allow them to support one another,

Figure 4-8.
You must eliminate the three guards in the west before you can cross the river.

so use caution. If they discover your men, they'll raise an alarm at the walled camp, so you may use your firearms if necessary.

Rather than just blast away the three soldiers, use this opportunity to fine-tune skills you'll need in later missions. All your Commandos begin near the southernmost building. The fence provides cover. Send the Green Beret and the Sapper to a point near the western opening in the fence. As Soldier 1 walks toward the river, send the Sapper to place the mantrap near the corner of the other building and hide around the corner. The enemy soldier will spot the Sapper's footprints in the snow and run to investigate. If the trap is in the correct position, the German will walk right into it and die. Then the Green Beret must rush in, grab the body, and hide it behind the fence before the other two enemy soldiers discover it. If, for some reason, the enemy misses the trap and discovers the Sapper, the Green Beret must act quickly and knife the enemy soldier as he trains his rifle on the Sapper.

Now to take out Soldier 2: The Sapper will need the trap again, so he must pick up the sprung trap and return to his hiding place. Observe Soldier 2's path. When he moves around the corner, place the trap in his path so Soldier 3 won't notice the body after the trap springs. After eliminating Soldier 2, recover the trap and move the Sapper back with the other Commandos.

Only one enemy soldier left. For this one you have a couple of options. Send the Green Beret out to knife Soldier 3 when he turns and walks away, and then carry the

Figure 4-9. After the Sapper places the trap, he runs behind the building. When the soldier sees the footprints, he'll come running—right into the trap.

Figure 4-10.
An enemy patrol boat motors up and down the river. If you hear its engine, take cover quickly. It's armed with dual machine guns.

body back behind the fence. Or use the Marine: Move him out a bit past the eastern opening in the fence so he leaves some footprints in the snow. Then run him back behind the fence. When the soldier sees the prints, he'll come running. As he moves through the opening, take him out with the speargun.

PHASE 2: INFILTRATE THE WALLED CAMP

In this phase your goal is to get all your Commandos into the walled camp unseen. Before you can cross the river, you must first eliminate any enemy soldiers who can observe the crossing point. Move your Sniper out the eastern opening in the fence to a position near the river. From there, bring up the precision rifle and target Soldier 4. Wait until he walks in front of the large rocks; then take him out. If you kill him anywhere other than where you see the '4' in figure 4-11, other enemy troops may spot the body and raise the alarm. Next, the Sniper must take out Soldier 5 (walking along the wall) near the ladder to prevent other soldiers from discovering the body.

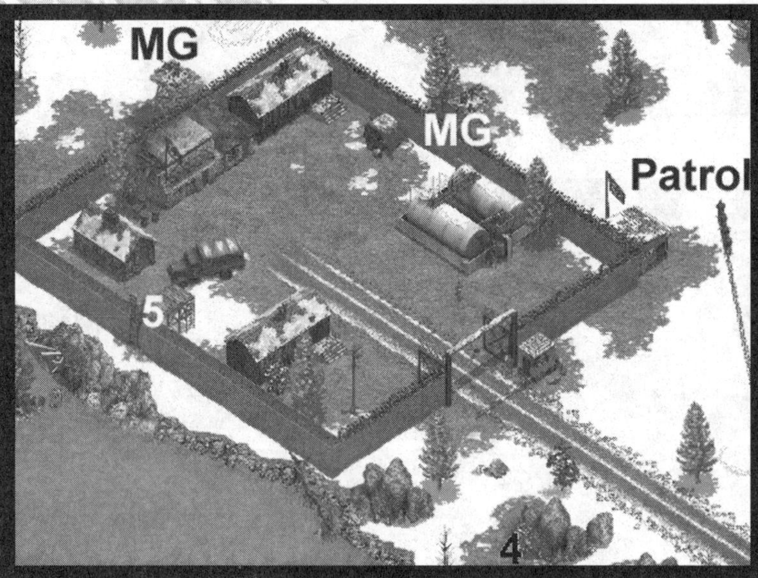

Figure 4-11.
This phase is easy. The key is to stay out of sight.

Now you're ready to cross the river. If the patrol boat hasn't come by lately, wait until it passes. Then move the Marine to the water's edge and inflate the raft. Row two Commandos across and go back for the other two. When everyone's on the opposite bank, deflate the raft (so the patrol boat won't spot it) and order all your men to lie prone behind the rock near the ladder where Soldier 5 died.

The ladder is your ticket into the camp, but the enemy's left it in the up position. The Green Beret can scale walls, however. Have him climb to the top, and then lower the ladder by clicking on it. Rush all your team members up the ladder and into the camp. Hide near the truck.

NOTE

Don't worry about the two machine-gun nests along the camp's northern walls. They face out, and can't fire into the camp. Avoid the temptation to take them out with your Sniper. Patrols outside camp will discover the gunners' dead bodies and sound the alarm.

Figure 4-12.
The Sniper takes out the guard on the camp wall from across the river.

PHASE 3: DESTROY THE FUEL DEPOT

Before you can plant the explosives, you must first clear the camp yard. When Soldier 6 begins marching toward the gate, send the Green Beret or Marine to knife him, and then silently kill Soldier 7, as well. When the patrol along the eastern map edge isn't looking, have this Commando raise the gate to make your getaway a little

TIP

Prepare your escape route before you place any explosives: the timers give you only 10 seconds. Also, watch the patrol along the eastern map edge. Don't start placing explosives until they're halfway along their northern march. When the explosives go off, they should be as far from the road as possible.

Figure 4-13.
Your men need to take out only two guards in this phase, unless an alarm sounds. Take care where you place the explosives.

easier. Now load all the Commandos, except the Sapper, aboard the truck. The Driver should move the truck to a position near the gate, but still within the camp walls.

When all is ready, send the Sapper to place the first explosive near the fuel depot. Set the second explosive near the camp wall's east corner. A guard barracks lies on the other side. The explosive will blast through the wall and destroy the barracks and the reinforcements within. Finally, get your Sapper onto the truck. Don't dawdle or the explosives will go off and take out the truck and all your Commandos. Once the Sapper is aboard, get the truck rolling. Double-click on your destination at the end of the road to order your Driver to drive fast. If all goes according to plan, you should be halfway down the road on your way to safety when the first explosion goes off.

TIP

Keep the truck moving right off the map. If you stop, the patrol along the eastern map edge will open fire and could kill all your Commandos before they can get away.

MISSION 3: REVERSE ENGINEERING

NORWAY, MARCH 4, 1941

It's March 1941. Repeated incursions in Norway are necessary to harass the occupation army and force Hitler to send troops to the zone, diverting them from the Mediterranean scenario. These incursions must meet minimum materiel needs and achieve maximum results.

This operation's objective is to demolish the large dam at Sysendam, near the Sima hydroelectric plant, in Eidfjord. This will take out several bridges and knock out electrical power to the whole area.

MISSION SUMMARY

Objective: Blow up the large dam.

Team: Green Beret, Marine, Sapper, Spy

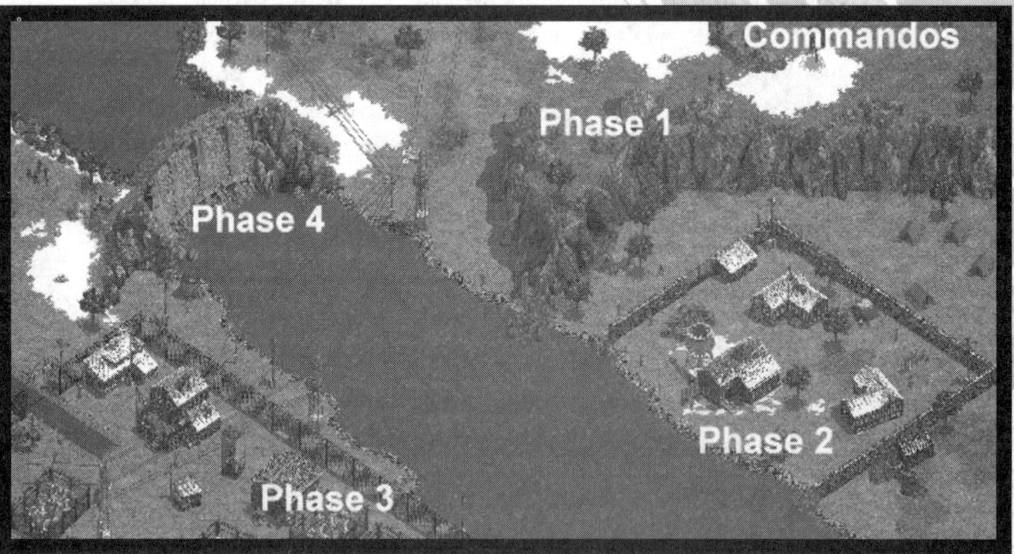

Figure 4-14. Reverse Engineering

Your team of four Commandos begins in the map's northeast corner. Your objective is straightforward, but achieving it is a little more complex. You must acquire explosives from a power station bounded by an electric fence, so you must find a German uniform for your Spy. You'll find one in the German camp on the east side of the river. After you destroy the dam, a truck will pick up your men east of the dam site.

PHASE 1: GET TO THE RIVER

Your team begins in the northeast, behind a wall. A patrol of three enemy soldiers (1, 2, and 3) will pass by your position. After they pass, send your Sapper to place the trap along the path of the German patrol. Then have the Green Beret place the decoy just west of the mantrap. Move both Commandos back behind the wall and wait for the patrol to return. Take control of the Green Beret so he can activate the decoy as soon as the mantrap kills an enemy soldier. This will distract the remaining two soldiers so the Marine can sneak up behind them and eliminate them quietly using the speargun.

Now order all your Commandos to run west into the little draw east of Soldier 4. The Green Beret should place the decoy at the western edge of the draw entrance and activate it to lure the soldier toward your team. Position the Marine so he has a good shot with the speargun and kill the enemy as he walks around the corner to look for you. Soldier 5 will spot the dead body eventually and come to investigate. Have the Marine take him out. Only Soldier 6 remains. Because he's looking out

Figure 4-15. In this phase, your men must kill six enemy soldiers on the way to the river.

Figure 4-16. Place the decoy and trap carefully for maximum effect.

over the river, this is an easy kill. Send the Marine down to take him out with either knife or speargun. Phase complete.

PHASE 2: ACQUIRING A GERMAN UNIFORM

Now that you've cleared a path to the river, you must get a German uniform for the Spy. One hangs on the clothesline in the camp on the river's east bank. The Marine will do all the killing in this phase. While the rest of the team hides in the draw, send the Marine into the river wearing his diving gear. Swim downriver past the German camp and wait as Soldier 7 approaches the wall. When he turns around, jump out of the river and kill him with the knife. Next, run along the south wall and watch for Soldier 8. He'll walk in among the tents and then head north again. As he does, run after him and kill him silently with the knife. Then return to the boat, pick it up, and enter the river.

Swim to the other side of the camp and quietly kill Soldier 9. Swim around the wall and wait near 10. When his back is turned, knife him, and then kill 11, as well.

Figure 4-17. Several enemy soldiers guard the uniform, located in the camp.

Return to the water, swim downstream to the other side of the rolls of cable, jump out, and run along the wall to knife Soldier 12. Follow the wall and knife 13. If you've avoided setting off an alarm, there's only one more German left. Soldier 14 is looking out over the river, so sneak up behind him and take him out.

Figure 4-18. The Spy finds a German uniform on the clothesline and puts it on.

Because the Marine can't pick up the uniform, he'll have to swim upstream to meet the Spy by the river's edge. Inflate the boat and row the Spy to the camp. Send the Spy to the clothesline, put on the uniform, and then row him back to the north coast. Drop off the Spy and pick up the Green Beret and Sapper. Row them back to the camp where you picked up the uniform and hide them in a building.

PHASE 3: GETTING THE EXPLOSIVES

Walk the German-uniformed Spy across the dam and right into the power station. The guards won't stop him. Walk over to the switch and flip it to deactivate the electric fence. Then walk down to talk to Soldier 17. Use the Distract command to keep his eyes away from the activity at the river.

The Marine must leave the boat behind for his next task. Put the diving gear back on and swim to the other side of the river near Soldier 15. Kill him with the speargun as close as possible to the map edge. Then swim to kill 16 at the southeast

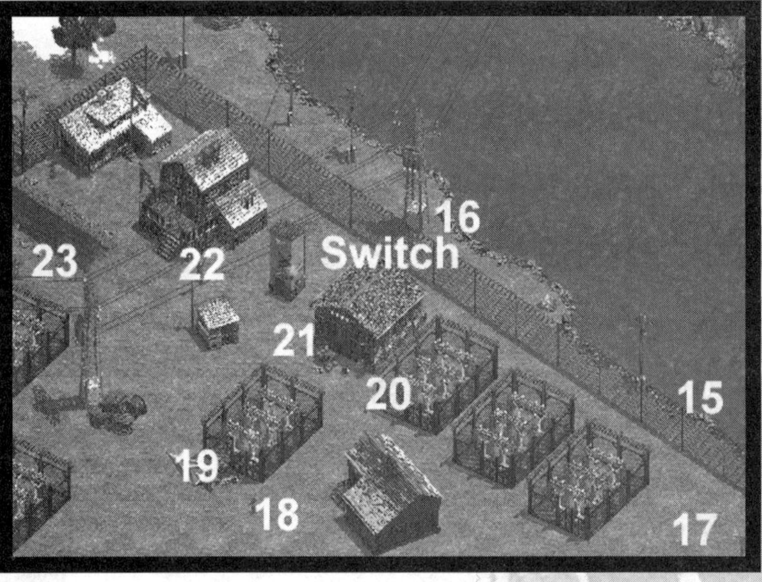

Figure 4-19. The power station is full of soldiers. Be careful: if the alarm sounds, even more will appear.

end of his patrol. Swim back to pick up the Green Beret and Sapper and row them across the river to a position near where you killed Soldier 15.

With the exterior guards dispatched, end the Spy's conversation and walk behind 17. Use the poison to keep Soldier 17 quiet—permanently. After the boat reaches shore, the Sapper must jump out and use the wire cutters to make an entrance in the fence. Then rush all the Commandos to hide behind the building near 18. Send the Spy to distract 18 while the Green Beret sneaks up behind and cuts his throat. The Green Beret must carry the body back behind the building so the other guards won't spot it. Now the Spy must go distract Soldier 23, near the main gate. Keep him looking at the gate so the Green Beret can knife 19 and dump the body behind the building. Now the Sapper can run and grab the first set of explosives.

Move the Sapper, Green Beret, and Marine along the bottom of the map toward the fence, and then up along the fence to hide behind the building near soldiers 20 and 21. Send the Spy to distract Soldier 22 while the Green Beret knifes 20 and 21 and hides their bodies behind the building. Now the Sapper can grab the second explosive and head back to the boat, along with the Marine.

You have both explosives now, but you still must clear out the remaining power station guards. Send the Spy back to talk to Soldier 23 while the Green Beret silently kills 22. Next, the Spy must distract Soldier 26. Keep an eye on 27: when he's not looking, the Green Beret can run in, kill Soldier 24, and remove the body. Repeat for 25.

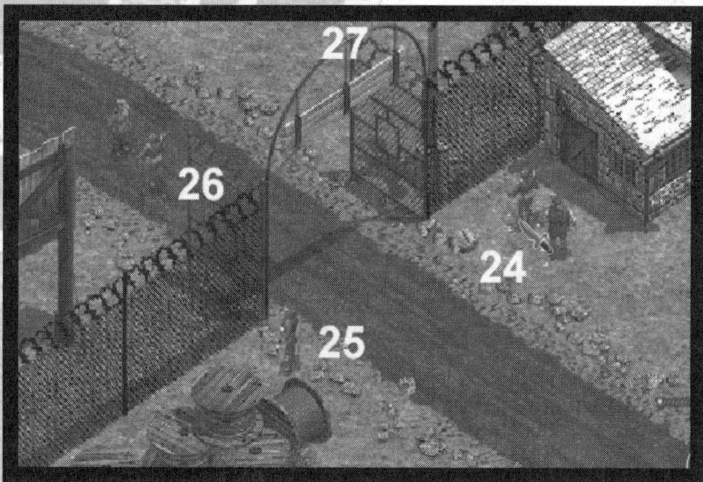

Figure 4-20. The Spy distracts enemy soldiers while the Green Beret sneaks around killing them.

WARNING

A patrol of four soldiers walks around the northwest map area. Keep an eye on them when killing guards near the front gate, because the patrol can see what's going on. Try using the split screen to monitor their movements while you carry out your tasks.

Now send the Spy to distract the patrol in the northwest part of the map. Keep the guards facing away from the main gate while the Green Beret kills soldiers 26 and 27. Conceal their bodies and head down to the boat, where the Marine and Sapper are waiting.

PHASE 4: BLOW UP THE DAM

Have the three Commandos row upstream to a position just south of the bunker near the dam. The Sapper must hop out, run behind the bunker, and place an explosive. Get him back in the boat as fast as possible; then row with the Marine to the other side of the river, near the German camp. When the explosive detonates, an alarm sounds, triggering reinforcements in the power station. The patrol stops talking to the Spy and heads to the river. Keep the boat out of their sight, or they'll fire on your Commandos.

After things cool down, use the Spy to distract any soldiers watching the dam. Then row the boat up next to the dam's base. The Sapper can jump out of the boat, place the explosive, and jump back in. Row to where the body of Soldier 6 lies and disembark all three Commandos. When the dam is damaged, a truck appears east of the dam. The Spy must cross the dam and board the truck with the rest of the team for the mission to end successfully.

Figure 4-21.
The Sapper places the explosive next to the bunker guarding the dam.

MISSION 4: RESTORE PRIDE

NORWAY, MARCH 10, 1941

In mid-March, German air raids on Britain accelerate. London, Liverpool, Glasgow, and other cities are heavily hit. Churchill understands the importance of successful incursions behind enemy lines for preserving the nation's morale.

The German military command in Trondheim has set their headquarters in a villa in nearby Stokkan. Your objective is to destroy the headquarters and wreak havoc in the zone.

MISSION SUMMARY

Objective: Blow up the German headquarters building.

Team: Green Beret, Sniper, Marine, Sapper, Driver

And you thought the last mission had a lot of enemy troops! More than 50 enemy soldiers, not counting reinforcements, stand ready to stop you in this mission. Your

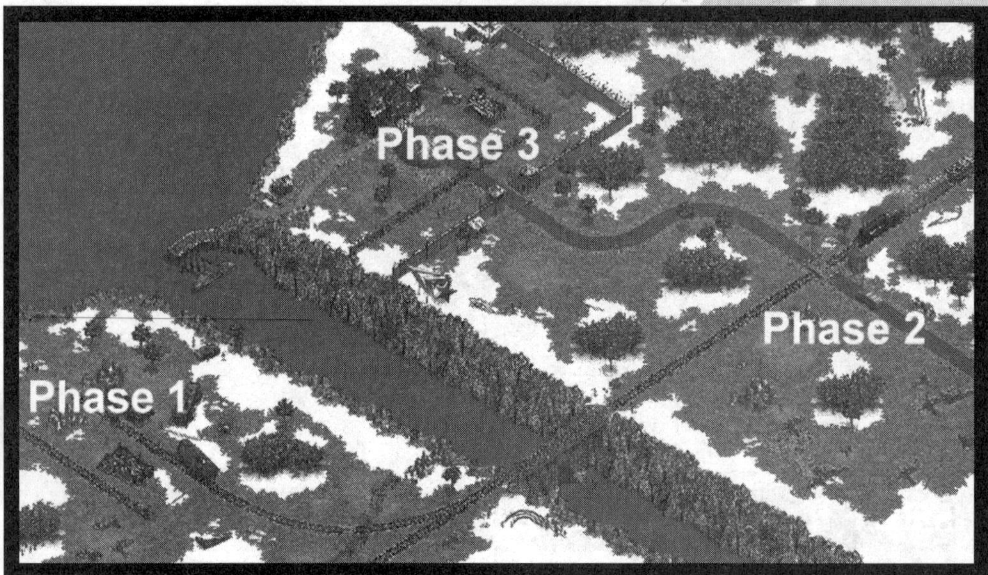

Figure 4-22. Restore Pride

team of five Commandos begins in the southwest map corner. You must first clear out the western area before crossing the railroad bridge over the fjord. Capturing the tank, if you can do it, will make your job much easier.

Once across the bridge, you must get to the supplies that were air-dropped in the woods to the northeast. With these supplies, you'll be ready to approach the headquarters behind the double walls. After you destroy it, all your Commandos must make it to the patrol boat at the dock, which will take them to safety.

PHASE 1: ADVANCE TO THE BRIDGE

This mission's five Commandos begin standing next to a small grove of trees in the southwest map corner. The first phase is the most difficult: they must eliminate 23 enemies before they can cross the bridge over the fjord safely. Many of the German soldiers are positioned to watch over one another, so sneaking up on them will be difficult. Start by putting all your men into a prone position.

Figure 4-23. You must kill 11 individual soldiers and a patrol to capture the tank. After that, this phase is a breeze.

NORWAY

The Green Beret will be the main man for the first part of this phase, and he'll do a lot of crawling. Three soldiers patrol the area immediately east of your start position. The Green Beret must crawl toward the building carefully—approaching from the west and out of Soldier 1's line of vision. When Soldier 3 begins walking east, take Soldier 1 out with the knife and move the body to the west side of the building, out of sight. Wait for Soldier 3 to finish his round and, when he turns away again, run up and knife Soldier 2, and then 3, quickly, the same way. Crawl back to where Soldier 1 stood and watch Soldier 4. You must kill him with the knife, as well, and remove the body. Use caution, however. Patrol 7 walks in a figure eight and at times has a good view of this area. Wait until they pass by before making your move.

TIP

The Sapper has only three grenades. You can use two during this phase, but save the third for the final phase.

Figure 4-24. The Sapper takes out the patrol with a grenade. He can take out three more soldiers with a second grenade if he waits a bit.

Continue, dispatching soldiers 5 and 6 the same way and moving their bodies behind the rock near where 6 stood.

By now the Green Beret's knife may need sharpening (and cleaning!). Keep him behind the rock with the bodies and have the Sapper crawl to this location. No, you're not going to have him set his trap. Instead, wait for Patrol 7 to come around. Lob a grenade at them (where you see the '7' on the map) to take out all three soldiers quickly. Other guards will hear the explosion and come to investigate. Don't worry, it's all part of the plan.

Soldiers 8, 9, and 10 should all leave their posts. When they walk close together, throw a second grenade in their midst. If you get only two with the grenade, that's fine. Take out the third with a pistol. Now the Green Beret can head east to take out soldiers 11, 12, and 13 silently. It's time to bring the Driver forward—but you might as well bring along the Marine and Sniper.

The Driver is the only team member who can drive the tank. To fire the tank's machine guns, control-click with the mouse. Drive toward Soldier 14 to kill him and

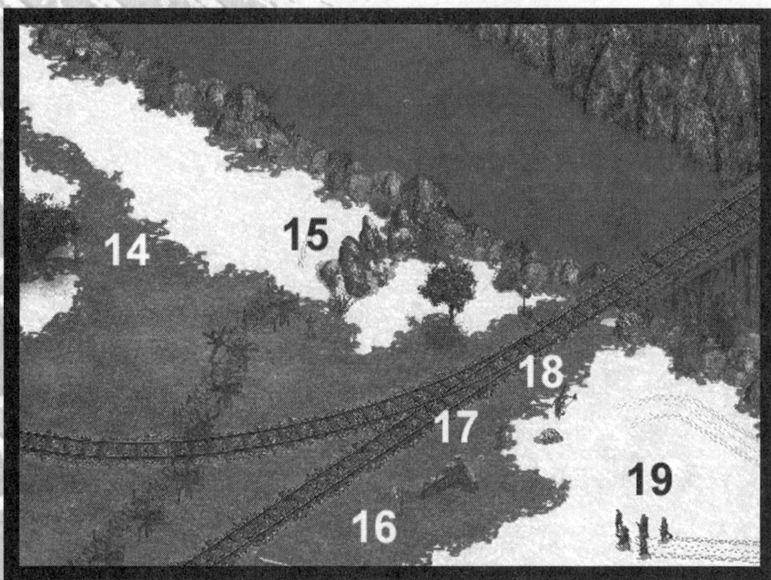

Figure 4-25.
Use the tank to clear out the rest of the enemy in Phase 1's area of operations.

15. Then move along the barbed-wire barrier, taking out soldiers 16 through 18 and Patrol 19. With the west side of the fjord clear, you're ready for Phase 2.

PHASE 2: GET THE SUPPLIES

Have the Driver train his sights across the fjord at Soldier 20. Take him out with a quick burst. Now wait a bit. Patrol 21 and Soldier 22 will see the body and come to investigate. With another couple of bursts, four more enemies are history. Now move your aim toward Soldier 23. You may have to move the tank up and down along the barbed wire a bit to hit him. After you do, wait for soldiers 24 and 26 and Patrol 25 to come and see. Take them out, as well.

Good job. You've killed 11 soldiers without even crossing the bridge.

TIP

The Marine should dump the boat before moving. You won't need it and it will only slow this Commando down.

Figure 4-26.
The long range of the tank's machine guns allows you to clear a large area on the east side of the bridge before your team crosses.

Figure 4-27.
Kill four more soldiers to clear the southeast section of the map.

It's time to move your team across the fjord. Have your Commandos gather near the opening in the barbed wire. Wait for the train to barrel over the bridge before quickly running your men across. If you hear the train coming, the ladder on the right-hand side of the bridge will keep a Commando from getting run over. (If you get caught on the tracks, your mission will come to a quick and unpleasant end.) Move the Commandos to a position south of the grove of trees near the body of Soldier 20 and his compatriots. Go prone. The Sniper must crawl to where he can take out the machine-gun nest (27) with the precision rifle. Then return him to the group. Next, the Green Beret must crawl southeast along the fjord to a point west of Soldier 28. Hide behind the rubble until he turns around; then knife him and soldiers 29 and 30.

Have the Green Beret crawl behind the building near the railroad crossing and wait. Make sure Patrol 33 is going away from the area and Soldier 32 is marching toward the eastern map edge before running to 31 and knifing him. Carry the body behind the grove of trees and quickly use the shovel to hide your Green Beret in the snow. Soldier 32 will come looking for you. When his back is turned, pop up out of the snow and take him out with the pistol.

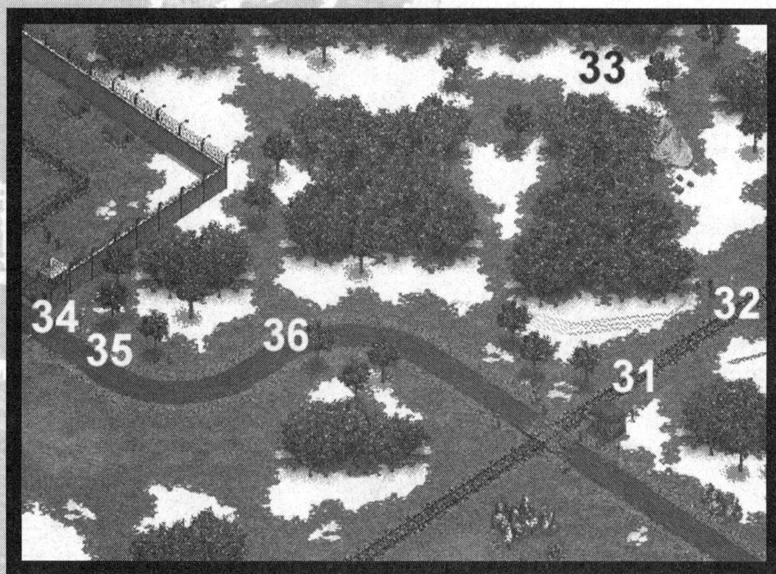

Figure 4-28. You need eliminate only five more soldiers and a patrol to complete Phase 2.

TIP

In Phase 3, you'll need a truck. From time to time one comes down the road and stops at the shack near the railroad crossing, where the driver gets out. Kill the driver and the truck is yours. It's an easy kill. The driver is unarmed and won't even yell if he sees your Commandos.

The coast is clear, so move the Sapper, Sniper, and Driver to where the Green Beret is waiting. Keep watch for Patrol 33. When it passes by and heads toward the air-dropped supplies, the three Commandos should follow. When they reach the supplies, the Driver must grab the machine gun quickly and run after the patrol. A quick burst takes out all three without alarming anyone. Now make sure the Sapper grabs the explosives and the Sniper the extra ammunition. The Sniper must carry this ammo along the railroad tracks toward the bridge. However, instead of crossing it, crawl toward the wall of the compound. Quickly take out soldiers 34 through 36 with the precision rifle to complete the phase.

PHASE 3: INFILTRATING THE HEADQUARTERS

Send the Driver to hop into the truck and drive it toward the main gate of the German headquarters. Move the rest of the men there, as well. While the Driver keeps the engine running, have the other Commandos crawl through the two gates and northeast along the wall to hide behind the building. Watch out for the patrol between the two walls. Move only when they turn away from the gate. Send all but the Sniper and the Sapper on to hide by the headquarters.

After the patrol turns around again, drive the truck through the first gate and stop it halfway through the second. The Driver must jump out quickly, before the patrol turns around and catches him in the truck. Move the Driver to the hiding place near the headquarters. Then move the Sapper forward so he can throw his last

Figure 4-29.
Phase 3 is easier than it seems. The trickiest part is getting the truck into the right position.

grenade at the truck. When it blows up, the flaming wreck will seal the interior gate and prevent reinforcements from getting into the main yard of the headquarters.

When the truck blows, soldiers 38 through 41 may come to investigate. The Driver should have no trouble taking them out with the machine gun. Move the Sniper along the wall toward Soldier 42 and drop him with the precision rifle; then take out the machine-gun nest (43). Mop up any remaining soldiers, including 44 by the boat, using the Driver's machine gun. Once it's clear, begin moving your team toward the patrol boat while the Sapper places explosives on the headquarters steps. Then get the Sapper to the patrol boat. Within 10 seconds, the mission objective will be in ruins. When all Commandos are on the patrol boat, it launches and carries your men to safety.

MISSION 5: BLIND JUSTICE

NORWAY, MAY 2, 1941

In May 1941, the Germans force Allied troops out of Crete and heavily bombard Liverpool and other British ports from the air. The need to turn Hitler's attention to Norway is greater than ever.

Your mission is to destroy a radar station near Herdla airfield. This will blind coastal defenses and give the occupation army a good reason to worry.

MISSION SUMMARY

Objective: Blow up the radar station in the mountaintop base.

Team: Green Beret, Spy

You have only two Commandos for this mission, but they can accomplish the objective. In the mission's first phase, you must get a uniform for the Spy and get both Commandos to the cable car. In the second, you must destroy the radar station in the mountain base using explosive barrels and escape in the autogyro.

Figure 4-30. Blind Justice

PHASE 1: GET TO THE CABLE CAR

Your Commandos begin in the northwest part of the map, behind a building. The Spy needs a uniform to reach the mountaintop. You'll find one near Soldier 8, but several other soldiers block your path. The Green Beret must clear the town. Remember to stay quiet. If the alarm sounds, the mission becomes nearly impossible to complete.

Start by moving the Green Beret west. Quickly place the decoy near the woods along the western map edge. Then hide in the hollow formed by the rocks. Soldier 1 will see your footprints in the snow and come to investigate. Activate the decoy to lure the soldier past you. While the device has him mesmerized, sneak up behind him and dispatch him with the knife. Keep an eye on Soldier 2. He also may hear the decoy and come looking. Knife him, as well. If he's oblivious to your actions and keeps patrolling, sneak up behind him and eliminate him silently. Next, take out Soldier 3. As he walks away from the Green Beret, run and knife him. Then carefully crawl behind Soldier 4 and kill him quietly. If you don't crawl, Soldier 8 will spot the Green Beret and ruin the surprise.

Now move the Green Beret to the building near Soldier 5. Wait until he begins walking away, and then run out from the building a bit to leave footprints where he can see them. Run back behind the building and use the shovel (press F) to hide in

Figure 4-31.
You must clear the town to gain access to the cable car.

the snow. Soldier 5 will come to investigate. When his back is turned, pop up and kill him with the knife. Now you can go after Soldier 6. Soldier 7 is next. His path takes him around the corner of a building. Take him out as far west as possible so no one will see.

Now the Green Beret must crawl south to the tree line, and then to the building near the telephone. Hide him in the building as you prepare for the next step. Move the Spy to a position near the grove of trees north of Soldier 8. Then press F3 to split the screen. Center the left side on the telephone near the Green Beret and the right on the phone near Soldier 8. When the patrol along the south map edge heads east, move the Green Beret out of the building and over to the telephone. He must wait until Patrol 19 begins walking toward Soldier 8 before calling. As soon as Soldier 8 heads for the phone, the Spy must run as fast as possible, grab the uniform, and put it on. Now the Green Beret can hang up and return to the safety of the building. Soldier 8 will return to his post. This allows the Spy to move behind him. When Patrol 19 heads southeast, use the lethal injection on Soldier 8 and carry his body behind the crates, out of the patrol's view.

Figure 4-32. Split the screen to monitor both telephones.

Figure 4-33.
You must eliminate all three guards around the cable car.

In the uniform, the Spy can walk all over the camp without arousing suspicion. Move toward Soldier 10 and distract him so he faces north. This permits the Green Beret to sneak up on Soldier 9 and knife him. Move the body behind the building to the south. Repeat with Soldier 10.

The Spy must distract Soldier 12 while the Green Beret kills Soldier 11. Then the Spy must distract Soldier 13 so the Green Beret can knife Soldier 12. Finally, the Spy can give Soldier 13 a lethal injection. To prepare for the next phase, the Green Beret should hide himself in the snow near where Soldier 11 was killed. The Spy can hop aboard the cable car and ride to the mountaintop.

PHASE 2: DESTROY THE RADAR STATION

When the Spy arrives atop the mountain, get out of the cable car and walk to Soldier 14. When he's not looking, poison him, and then walk over to and behind Soldier 15. Watch Patrol 18. As they walk past you going north, quickly kill 15 with the lethal injection and carry the body behind the barracks near Soldier 16. After dumping the body, run to the patrol and distract them until the Spy's footprints leading to the body disappear. Next kill Soldier 16 and dispose of his body in the same place as 15. Move the Spy back to the cable car and head back down the mountain to pick up the Green Beret.

Figure 4-34. The mountaintop base isn't heavily guarded, but an alarm will bring several more soldiers out of the barracks.

As the cable car moves, split the screen again. Keep the right side on Patrol 19 and the left on the cable car at the bottom of its line. When Patrol 19 heads toward the mountain, rush the Green Beret into the cable car and move it back up to the top. Patrol 19 can see the Green Beret at the top station, so act quickly: The Spy must run up to Patrol 18 and distract them so the Green Beret can crawl over near the explosive barrels and hide himself in the snow. The Spy must continue distracting the patrol until the Green Beret's footprints disappear.

The next part is tricky, so save your game here.

The Spy must walk over to Soldier 17. Wait until Patrol 18 reaches the northernmost point of its route and turns south. Quickly poison 17 and then run down to distract Patrol 18. Keep them south of the barrels, looking south. This allows the Green Beret to pop up and move the barrels around unnoticed. Place one barrel a little closer to the front of the barracks and another barrel next to the radar dish. Place the third barrel anywhere you wish. After he positions all the barrels, move the Green Beret north and dig him into the snow a little south of the autogyro.

Figure 4-35.
The Spy distracts the patrol while the Green Beret moves the explosive barrels around the base.

NOTE

To give the Green Beret a real workout, or if the Spy doesn't feel like taking another cable car ride, the Green Beret can use his muscles to scale the mountainside. The base of the mountain is mined in some areas, so move cautiously. Wait until the southern patrol heads east and run after them, careful to stay in their footprints. Before they reach the place where they turn around, dig the Green Beret into the snow to hide. Continue paying close attention to the patrol. At the point where they end their eastward march, they make a wide turn. A mine lies within that arc. By the time they pass over the hidden Green Beret, their footprints probably will have disappeared, so you must remember where they walked and follow their path. Also, make sure the Spy has eliminated Soldier 16 before you begin your climb, or the Green Beret won't have a lot of fun at the top. The Spy also must distract Patrol 18 until the Green Beret can find a hiding spot at the top.

Now the Spy can end his conversation with the patrol and stand so he can shoot the pistol at the barrel next to the barracks. Don't bring up the gun until he's ready to fire. If you wait until the patrol is next to the barrel before firing, you can take them out at the same time. Put the gun away immediately after firing in case reinforcements make it out of the barracks. Kill those who do by shooting barrels as they pass by. Be sure to shoot the barrel next to the radar dish. Then get both Commandos to the autogyro, which flies them to safety.

MISSION 6: MENACE OF THE LEOPOLD

NORWAY, MAY 10, 1941

Norwegian spring advances. The Germans are preparing for next month's attack on the Soviet Union, Operation Barbarossa. Several tests are underway in Norway.

As part of this rehearsal, they will use the long-range Leopold cannon against the Norwegian Resistance before carrying it to the eastern front. Your mission is to shut down this dangerous weapon.

MISSION SUMMARY

Objective: Destroy the Leopold cannon.

Team: Green Beret, Sniper, Sapper

Your three-Commando team begins in the northwest. Because of the map's size and enemy's numbers (this mission is crawling with Germans), the mission has five phases. First, you must enter the compound through the bombed-out structure near your starting position. Once inside, you must make your way through the German base to the Leopold cannon. However, before blowing it up, you should clear an avenue of escape. German headquarters lie south of the cannon. Avoid it, and the soldiers near it, or an alarm will sound and ruin the mission. Until you destroy the cannon, you don't want the enemy to know you're there.

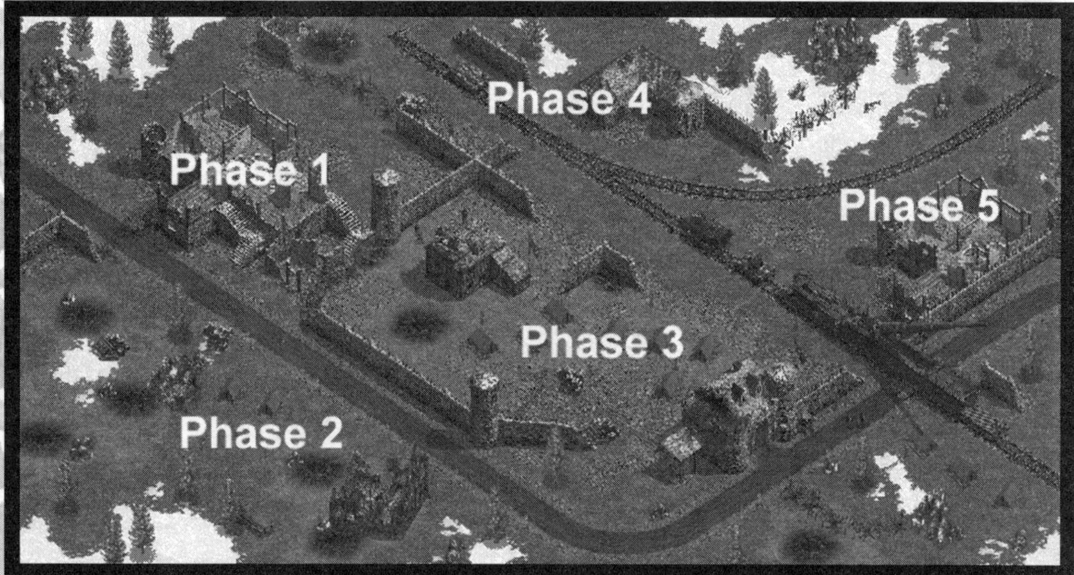

Figure 4-36. Menace of the Leopold

PHASE 1: INFILTRATE THE OUTER DEFENSES

Your Commandos all begin in the northwest, but the first phase requires only the Green Beret. Start by watching Soldier 1. When he turns and heads away from you, run after him and give him the blade. Then crawl over to the wall of the building below Soldier 2. Scale the wall with the pick and dispatch him silently with the knife. Time this so Soldier 3 isn't looking when you make your move. Quickly move his body behind the clock before the other guards see it. Soldier 3 will come back around, but when he turns to walk away, run after him and take him down. Now move back to where you entered the building and descend the wall.

Move around the structure to the ladder at the east entrance. Climb it and take out Soldier 4 when 5 isn't looking. Quickly carry the body behind a wall and then go after soldiers 5 and 6. Just leave their bodies where they drop. Now the Green Beret can take out Soldier 7, while watching for 9, and move the body out of sight. After killing 7 and 8, and moving their bodies, place the decoy where 8 was. Conceal yourself behind the wall to the north and turn on the decoy. Both soldiers 9

Figure 4-37.
Your team enters the German base through this building filled with enemy soldiers.

and 10 will come to investigate, allowing you to take them both out while their backs are turned.

PHASE 2: APPROACHING THE INNER COMPOUND

Have the Green Beret crawl south toward the rocks. Wait for the half-track to pass, and then kill Soldier 11. Carry the body out of sight behind the rocks. Let the half-track pass again and repeat with Soldier 12. While this is taking place, begin moving the Sniper and Sapper into the base though the building the Green Beret just cleared. Position the Sniper near where Soldier 9 patrolled and move the Sapper over by the Green Beret. After the half-track passes again, have the Sapper run out and place an explosive near 13 (see figure 4-38). After it's set, return to hide behind the rocks. When the half-track moves near the explosive, set it off with the detonator. The explosion takes place far enough from headquarters that no alarm sounds.

Figure 4-38.
There aren't many enemies to kill in this phase, but you must cross a lot of open ground and deal with an armed half-track.

However, soldiers from the inner compound, usually 14 and 15, come to look. Take control of your Sniper and bring up the scope on the precision rifle. Wait until both guards cross the road and then take them out. You've just made Phase 3 a little easier. If more guards come to investigate, you can take out one more, but you must save two bullets for later in the mission.

PHASE 3: CLEARING THE INNER COMPOUND

The Sniper leads this phase. Order him to crawl south and then east along the southern map edge until he can take a shot at Soldier 16 atop the headquarters building. Then crawl and shoot Soldier 17. As the Sniper does this, move the Green Beret and Sapper up to the turret near the Sniper. After the Sniper conducts his business, the Green Beret can take the lead again.

First, crawl to Soldier 18 and take him down. Next, crawl northeast and around behind Soldier 19. However, before killing him, watch Patrol 21. Wait until they head back west before making your move. Carry the body behind a railroad car so the patrol doesn't discover it when they come back around. Now the Green Beret can sneak up behind Soldier 20 and kill him.

Figure 4-39.
This phase is fairly easy, but a careless mistake could bring soldiers pouring out of the barracks to kill your Commandos.

PHASE 4: CLEAR THE AVENUE OF ESCAPE

Again watching Patrol 21, run over with the Green Beret to the wall southwest of 22. Wait until Soldier 23 heads away from you before killing 22; then quickly run after 23 and kill him, too. Before making a move on 24, take a look at Soldier 25. When he heads southeast, move fast. Take out 24 and carry the body behind the wall. Then, staying behind cover, move next to the building near 25 and wait for him to walk away again. The Green Beret must run as fast as he can and knife soldiers 25 and 26. Catch your breath and order all Commandos to crawl to point X in figure 4-41.

PHASE 5: DESTROY THE LEOPOLD CANNON

Yes, you're itching to blow up the cannon, but let's take out four more soldiers first, or your truck out of here may be destroyed before you can hop aboard. Take time to observe soldiers 27 through 29 and notice that it's impossible to approach any of them without being spotted by one of the others. Time for the Green Beret to get out his trusty decoy. Place it near the turret west of Soldier 29.

Figure 4-40.
Before you blow up the Leopold cannon, make sure you can escape.

Figure 4-41.
You must clear one more building before the fireworks start.

With the decoy in place, the Green Beret can crawl over to the ladder leading into the structure. But before climbing it, watch Soldier 29. At times he can see the platform, so you must time it just right. Once you're up the ladder, crawl to the right side of the platform. When Soldier 27 walks away, move quickly to the

Figure 4-42. Place the decoy near the turret to distract soldiers 28 and 29.

southeast corner. Then, while 29 looks away, move northeast to hide behind the wall. Now activate the decoy. Wait until both 28 and 29 look away to sneak up on 27 and knife him. Take out 28 and 29 in quick succession before they lose interest in the decoy. Now the Green Beret can shut it off before it drives you crazy. Descend the ladder and run to the machine gun (30) and take it out. Move the Green Beret and Sniper to a position on the railroad tracks east of the machine gun. Staying near the machine gun may get your Commandos run over by their ride out of here.

It's time: have the Sapper place the last explosive next to the Leopold cannon and then run to join the rest of the team. With all three Commandos down on the ground, detonate the explosives and watch the fireworks. Quickly drag a box around your team as you hold down the right mouse button to group them and wait for the getaway truck. When it arrives, move your Commandos to it as quickly as they can run. The truck will take some fire, so the faster you get it out of range, the better.

Now take a break. After all this, you probably need one.

MISSION 7: CHASE OF THE WOLVES

NORWAY, FEBRUARY 7, 1942

On February 1, 1942, the Germans shift to a new cipher code to communicate with their U-boats, the dreaded submarines that threaten vital convoys feeding Britain. This means the Allies have lost one of their most powerful weapons—the ability to decode German messages.

According to one of the last deciphered communications, a group of U-boats is making an intermediate stop at the Norwegian port of Arendal. Your orders are to infiltrate the U-boat shelter and sabotage the submarines.

MISSION SUMMARY

Objective: Set off explosives on the two submarines at dock.

Team: Green Beret, Marine, Sapper, Driver, Spy

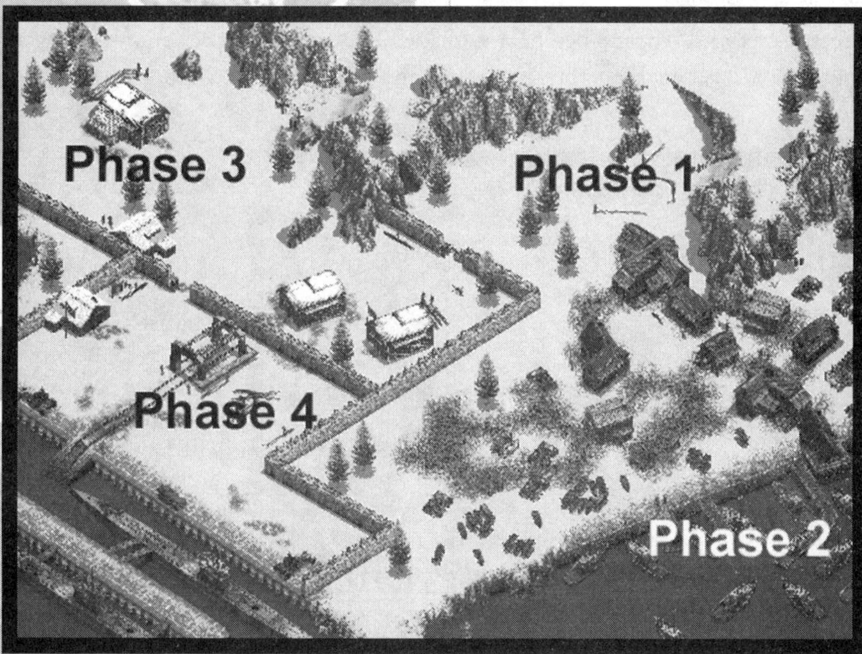

Figure 4-43. Chase of the Wolves

As you begin, your force comprises two groups. The Sapper, Driver, and Spy, in the west, have managed to infiltrate the base. Their job is to sabotage the two U-boats at dock. The Green Beret and Marine, in the northeast, outside the German base, must provide a means of escape for the first group. The village marina in the southeast has a small rowboat.

The mission takes place in four phases: First, the Green Beret and Marine must clear the area where they begin so they can advance to the second phase—taking out all opposition in and around the village and grabbing the boat. In Phase 3, the other group of Commandos must obtain the air-dropped explosives. Finally, they infiltrate and clear the dockyard before sabotaging the U-boats.

The mission is daunting, but take it one step at a time and you'll do fine. Save your game often. Some steps involve a lot of waiting and walking.

PHASE 1: OUTSIDE THE VILLAGE

The Green Beret and Marine begin in a pickle. They're hiding behind a rock with four enemy soldiers blocking their way into the village. Take a quick look at the

Figure 4-44. The Green Beret and Marine work together to take out the four soldiers blocking access to the village.

guards' locations and paths. When Patrol 3 and Soldier 1 both head west, send the Marine running north. Drop prone just as Soldier 1 begins turning; then crawl west as far as possible.

Have the Green Beret use the shovel to hide himself in the snow while the Marine makes tracks. Soldier 1 will see the Marine's footprints in the snow and go to investigate. When he passes the Green Beret, send your man after him and take the German out with the blade as the enemy heads west. Bring the Green Beret back to the rock and wait for soldiers 2 and 3 to turn west again. Then order your man to run south to the gap between the rocks and the building and hide in the snow there. Soldier 2 will see the footprints and come to investigate. When he gives up and begins to leave, pop up and knife him. Move the body farther south if it lies where Patrol 3 can spot it.

Now carefully bring the Marine back down to where he started the mission. The Green Beret must place the decoy near the snowy slope east of where Soldier 1 patrolled—without the patrol spotting him. Then have him run back south to the gap. Don't hide him in the snow or he won't be able to activate the decoy. When the patrol approaches the decoy, start it singing. When both guards are staring at it, move the Marine in for the kill.

This requires a quick hand and some practice, so it's a good idea to save the mis-

TIP

Of all the Commandos, the Marine has the best chance of killing a two-guard patrol quickly and silently. But this takes practice. The key is to approach the patrol from the rear and use the knife on the closest soldier. No matter how well you do, the other soldier will turn around. Immediately after using the knife, then, the Marine must bring up the speargun. Press J for this and fire at the second enemy. If you don't use the hotkey, the second enemy will sound an alarm and probably start shooting. If you shoot the first and try to knife the second, you must close on the second enemy, giving him plenty of time to respond to the cry of his compatriot, turn, and kill you instead. Master this skill and you can use it in other missions, including multiplayer.

sion here with a quicksave (Ctrl + S). You must move over to knife the rear enemy, quickly bring up the speargun (J), and then shoot the second enemy before he can turn and shoot you.

PHASE 2: CLEAR THE VILLAGE

Move the Marine down to the gap with the Green Beret. Then send the Green Beret around the west side of the building. When Soldier 4 turns away, run south a bit, to leave some tracks, and then a bit north, to hide in the snow. Soldier 4 will come to see who made the tracks. When he heads back toward his post, pop up and knife him. Carry the body back slightly, out of sight of other soldiers. Next, keep an eye on Patrol 8 as you take out Soldier 5 as he and the patrol walk east. Remove the body to where you dropped 4. Just so the Marine doesn't get bored, send him first to kill 6 with his choice of silent weapons, and then to hide in the building near where 4 patrolled.

The next step is tricky. When no one is looking, move the Green Beret into the building near Soldier 5's post. Then, when Patrol 8 moves east and Soldier 7 is walk-

Figure 4-45. The village contains several German soldiers and a barracks. Taking out the barracks prevents reinforcements from causing more trouble.

Figure 4-46.
Soldier 9 and Patrol 10 will come to the aid of the exploded barracks. Try to kill the patrol while they're in the village. Otherwise, you'll have to take out all four soldiers at the marina, where they can support one another.

ing northeast, quickly jump out, run after 7, and knife him. Immediately, grab the body and carry it north to the barrels. Drop the body, pick up a barrel, and hide the body under it. Then dig a hole in the snow for cover before the patrol can spot you.

When the patrol again heads east, move the Marine into the building where the Green Beret was and order the Green Beret to carry the barrel down to the barracks' west corner. Drop the barrel. Then move back a bit so the patrol can't see you, but you have a clean shot at the barrel with the pistol. When the patrol walks next to the barracks, shoot the barrel. It will explode, taking out both the barracks and the patrol. A single soldier may come out of the barracks, so hide in the snow or move the Green Beret around the building and out of sight.

In response to the explosion, Soldier 9 and Patrol 10 may come to assist. Watch them carefully. Take out the patrol, at least, with the Marine's silent double-kill skill. If you can, though, get Soldier 9 while he's in the area. Otherwise, take him out at his post on the pier. Now, to get to the rowboat, you need only sneak up on Soldier 11 and take him out silently. Send the Marine down to the rowboat. The Green Beret still has a patrol to kill—Patrol 12, near the lighthouse.

Carry the second explosive barrel southwest along the wall to the German base; then hide behind the corner of the wall until the patrol heads back toward the lighthouse. Move the barrel to a point along their route and then hide in the snow. You may have to move the barrel a bit and then hide more than once so you

aren't caught. Position the Green Beret so he can pop up and shoot the barrel as the patrol walks near it. They won't hear the explosion in the base if the patrol isn't near the wall. Finally, position the Green Beret on the other side of the wall from Soldier 17 (see figure 4-48).

PHASE 3: RETRIEVE THE EXPLOSIVES

This is a short and easy phase. The Spy begins by crawling around the building toward the gate into the dockyard. Keep an eye on Patrol 13, to the east. When Soldier 15 heads away from you, and the patrol in the yard isn't looking, quickly run and grab a German uniform. When the guard turns around, he'll see a German officer instead of a Spy.

Have the Spy approach Patrol 14 and distract them with conversation of his choice while the Sapper crawls to the air-dropped crate and retrieves the explosives. Keep the Spy talking until the Sapper's footprints disappear. While the Sapper and Driver wait by the building where they began the mission, the Spy can move back over to the dockyard gate, ready for the next phase.

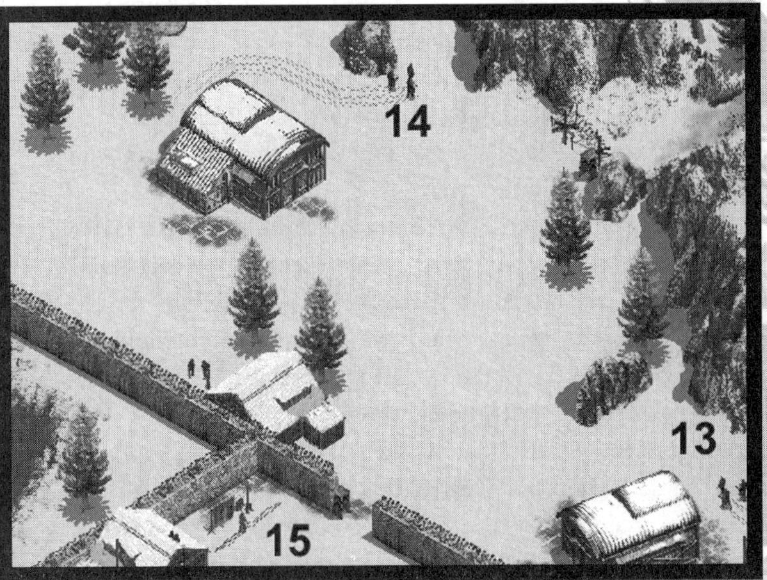

Figure 4-47. You needn't kill a single enemy soldier in Phase 3. Don't worry, Phase 4 makes up for it.

PHASE 4: SABOTAGING THE U-BOATS

This phase isn't difficult, but it requires a lot of waiting, timing, and walking with dead bodies. The Spy begins by walking over to Soldier 15 (who couldn't guard a clothesline of laundry) and giving him a lethal injection. Carry the body out the gate and dump it near the door of the building east of the gate. Before you pull out the syringe, make sure Patrol 21 is turned away, beginning their walk east. You must be wary of this patrol throughout the rest of this phase. Waiting until they begin their eastward march gives the Spy enough time to dispose of the bodies at the aforementioned building.

Next, have the Spy walk over to Soldier 16. Soldier 17 is in view, so have the Green Beret, already in position, activate the decoy to distract him while the Spy

TIP

To complete this mission in good time, after he distracts Soldier 17 with the decoy, have the Green Beret run back to the rowboat and the Marine will row it west and around the lighthouse jetty. Take care to stay out of sight of Gun 23.

Figure 4-48. A lot of soldiers mill about this small area. To clear out the dockyard, you must have patience and tenacity.

kills 16 quietly and takes care of the body. Shut off the decoy once the Spy is safe. Repeat with soldiers 17, 18, and 19, in that order.

Now comes the hard part, so save the mission here. The Spy must walk over to Soldier 20 and wait for Patrol 21 to pass, headed east. Quickly kill Soldier 20, and then run after the patrol. You must reach the end of their march before they do and distract them as close as possible to Gun 23. You want the patrol next to the gun, with the Spy a bit farther off.

You finally get to use the Driver. While Patrol 21 is distracted by the Spy, do the following: Make the Sapper and the Driver crawl into the dock facility. Send the Driver to the half-track and the Sapper down to Gun 22. Drive the half-track just west of the dock structure so it's out of the sight of Gun 23, but still has a clear shot at the barracks. Have the Sapper place a time bomb at Gun 22, then run to the half-track for cover. As soon as the bomb explodes, troops will pour out of the barracks. Mow them down with the half-track's machine guns. After all the troops in the barracks have been killed, move the half-track near the wall where Soldier 17 patrolled.

Figure 4-49. The Driver in the half-track mows down the reinforcements coming from the barracks.

Figure 4-50. Place the explosives on the stern of the U-boats near the torpedoes.

Have your Spy end the conversation and allow the patrol to return. As they come within sight of the bodies they will go on alert, but not for long. As they become visible, take them out with the half-track. Once the coast is clear, have the Sapper exit the half-track and blow up Gun 23.

After the reinforcements stop coming, unload the Driver and Sapper and send them and the Spy to the ramp near Soldier 20's body. The Marine must row over to them (don't forget the Green Beret), pick them up, and then row to the platform at the east end of the dock, between the two U-boats. Here the Sapper can disembark and climb the ladder. Run to either U-boat and plant an explosive at the stern, near the waiting torpedoes. Repeat on the remaining U-boat. If you fail to plant the explosives next to the torpedoes, no chain reaction will take place and the damage will be superficial. After placing the explosives, run back to the boat. The mission ends once the Marine rows all Commandos to the red buoy in the map's southeast corner.

CHAPTER 5

THE NORTH AFRICAN CAMPAIGN

With the British now fighting Axis forces in North Africa, your team has been called from Norway to assist in driving the Germans and Italians out. The Commandos must trade their warm clothing for something much cooler. Gone is the snow, replaced by sand. As with snow, walking across sand leaves tracks. It's also easy for the Green Beret to hide in the sand.

This campaign's five missions are more difficult than those you faced in Norway. Except for Mission 9, the maps crawl with enemy soldiers. You must take special care and use the skills you honed in the previous seven missions. Good luck.

MISSION 8: PYROTECHNICS

NORTH AFRICA, OCTOBER 19, 1942

Now that General Montgomery has arrived at El Alamein, tense preparations are underway in both British lines and Rommel's German–Italian lines. The battle of El Alamein is about to begin.

In the meantime, the Commandos will lead small incursions against Rommel's positions. Today's orders are to attack a supply center in Tell el Eisa. If you succeed, it will leave a whole armored division without supplies.

MISSION SUMMARY

Objective: Blow up the water tower and fuel storage tanks at the German supply depot.

Team: Green Beret, Sniper

This is another tough mission. The small map is crawling with enemy soldiers and you have only two Commandos. But they're all you need to complete the mission.

Your team begins in the northwest, in the ruins on the plateau overlooking the German supply depot. The mission has four phases. The first requires you to clear the plateau of enemy troops. Next, infiltrate the enemy base. Once you're in, you must clear out the defenders and prepare to destroy the objectives as part of Phase 3. Finally, your team must prepare their escape route and blow up the water and fuel supply.

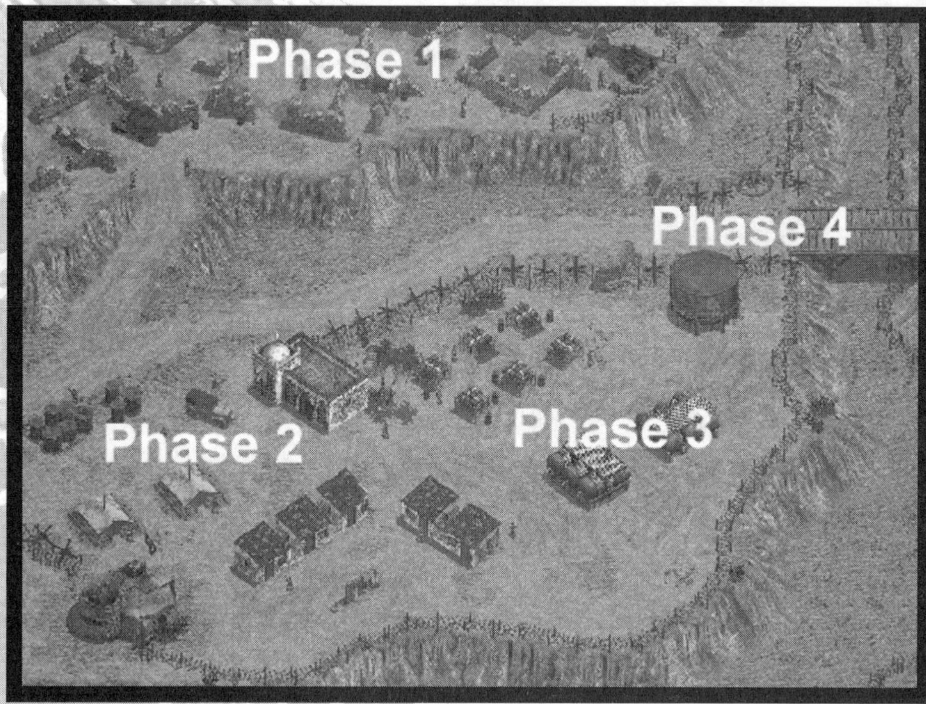

Figure 5-1. Pyrotechnics

Stay alert during this mission. Before you kill a guard, make sure no one can see you. As usual, save the mission often: it doesn't take much for these veteran soldiers to sound the alarm.

PHASE 1: CLEAR THE PLATEAU

Your team begins surrounded by the enemy. Order the Sniper to lay prone while the Green Beret crawls and places the decoy behind the wall to the north. Crawl back to the corner where you started and activate the decoy. Soldier 1 will walk toward it. After he passes the prone Green Beret, take him out with the knife and put the body next to the decoy. Now move the decoy to the south side of the same wall and return to the hiding spot. Activate the decoy to lure Soldier 2 away from his post so you can knife him, as well. Then pick up the decoy and place it near 2's post and activate it. Soldier 3 will come to investigate. Kill him silently and take the body out of the area.

Now the Sniper can crawl to where Soldier 3 stood while the Green Beret returns to the starting area. With the precision rifle, the Sniper can take out

Figure 5-2. Because many of the soldiers can see one another, you must use the decoy to lure them into your ambushes, out of others' view.

Soldier 4, which allows the Green Beret to sneak up behind 5 and use his knife. Move all the bodies out of sight.

Carefully crawl the Green Beret to the gap just north of Soldier 12. Soldier 6 is your next target. Wait until he turns around, and then run after him with the knife. (Time your approach for when 7 isn't watching.) Move the body into the alcove north of Soldier 6's post. Take a breather, wipe off the blade and get ready for the next part of the phase.

Keeping an eye on 8 and 13, move in behind Soldier 7, knife him, and quickly carry the body out of sight. When 8 turns his back, run after him and stick a blade in him. Again, dispose of the body accordingly. When Soldier 10 turns away, run and kill him. After killing 10, place the decoy next to the barrel. Hide. Turn on the decoy and wait for soldiers 9 and 11 to investigate. Knife them when they have their backs turned. Hide their bodies. Do the same with 11, and then move the body before the other soldiers spot it.

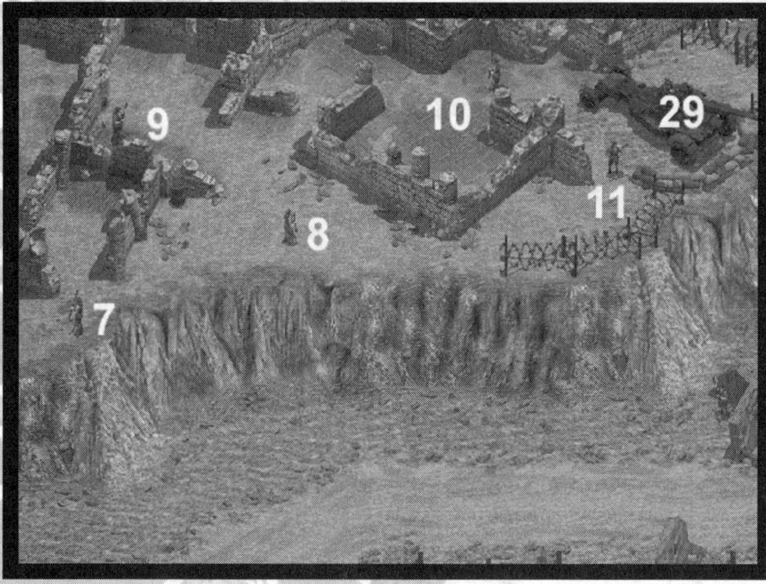

Figure 5-3.
The enemies are spread out a bit in the second half of Phase 1.

Now move the Green Beret back toward the Sniper. Place the decoy west of Soldier 13, and then crawl so the Green Beret is right behind 12. Split the screen to keep an eye on Soldier 14 at the base of the plateau (see figure 5-4). Activate the decoy, and when 13 turns to look at it, kill 12 and remove the body. Shut off the decoy, move in behind 13, take him down, and carry the body out of sight.

PHASE 2: INFILTRATE THE GERMAN SUPPLY BASE

Time to wake up the Sniper. Move him west to the map edge, and then south to the edge of the plateau. Target Soldier 14 and drop him at the western end of his route so no one can see the body. Quickly put the Sniper back on the ground while the Green Beret crawls down the slope to 14's body. When 15 heads east, move into the gap in the oil drums, keeping a close eye on 16 as you go. After 15 passes you going the other direction, run after him, take him out with the knife, and carry the body over to the tent where 18 stands guard.

Crawl back toward the plateau and place the decoy in the middle of the road near the base of the ascending slope. Hide in the gap in the oil drums and activate the decoy. Soldier 16 will leave his post. When his back is turned, kill him and drag the body to the drums.

Figure 5-4. Be careful in this base. Everybody can see just about everybody else.

The Green Beret must *not* move into the open. Crawl so you're positioned just north of Soldier 17; watch soldiers 23, 24, and 28. When all march away from you, knife 17 and quickly carry his body around to the tent where you dropped off 14's remains. Then approach and kill 18 and move the body, watching for 20 the entire time. Crawl over near 20 and, when he turns, hide in the westernmost little building.

Move the Sniper to the oil tanks and take aim at Soldier 19, on the barracks roof. When 26 isn't watching, take out 19.

Back to the Green Beret. When 21 and 22 both walk away, knife 20 and hide the body west of the building. The Green Beret must now make his way carefully to the northwestern building of the two near 21. You may have to hide in buildings along the way to avoid being spotted.

Bring the Sniper crawling down the slope, and then toward the southwest barracks. Position him so he can take a shot at Soldier 22 at the south end of his patrol. The Green Beret must wait until 21 passes by his door, moving southeast. Jump out and knife him. Then hit the dirt. The Sniper can then drop 22 as he rounds the corner; the Green Beret must quickly move the body over near 21's. Move the Sniper to the oil drums near 14. Have the Green Beret place the decoy west of bodies 21 and 22, but just out of sight of 24. Activate it and hide in the nearby building. Soldier 23 will come to investigate. Knife him when his back is turned, and then hide the body.

PHASE 3: PREPARING FOR A BIG EXPLOSION

Have the Green Beret crawl to the north side of the barracks where 19 patrolled on the roof. The Sniper must crawl to the same area, but will have to find a good position to target Soldier 30 (see figure 5-6). After he shoots, move the Sniper into the gap in the oil drums.

Soldier 24 will see 30's body and go to investigate. The Green Beret must kill him as he rounds the corner. To get at the soldiers on the fuel tanks, you must first take out Soldier 25. Crawl east from the barracks and place the decoy behind 25, on the other side of the barbed wire. Move back by the barracks and activate the decoy. To reach it, 25 must come around, as 24 did. Use the same procedure and kill another German.

You're almost there. Move the Green Beret back into the base and have him make his way around to 21's former post. When 26 heads north, run to the ladder

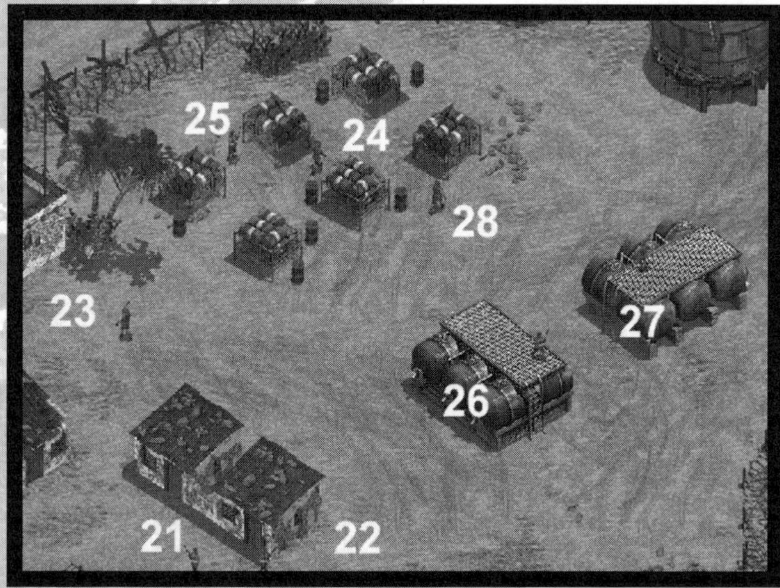

Figure 5-5. Don't the German guards know how volatile those barrels and tanks can be?

Figure 5-6. Placing the explosive barrels correctly is important. You get only one chance to set off the chain reaction.

at the base of the fuel tanks. Wait until he moves north again; then climb the ladder quickly and take him down with the knife. Climb down and do the same with 27 when 28 isn't looking. Finally, kill 28 as he walks away from you. Move his body in among the fuel barrels to hide it from other guards.

TIP

To wipe out some of the enemy's reinforcements at the same time you take out the rest of the supply base, carry the two explosive barrels at the top of the slope down to the white barracks. Place one at the east corner of the building and the other near the racks of barrels to the east. This just adds a few more dominoes to the line.

Now comes the fun part. Although you could blow all the objectives now, you'd still have to escape through the base—not a good idea: reinforcements will pour out of the barracks after the first explosion. Instead, you must set up a chain of explosions you can detonate from *outside* the base. Position the barrels as in figure 5-6. Then you need only fire a pistol (from the other side of the barbed wire) at the barrel near the water tank. When the barrels are set to go, send both Commandos to meet at the white barracks.

PHASE 4: THE CRESCENDO

This mission has been a lot of hard work, but it will pay off in spades. The Sniper should make his way cautiously to hide behind the wall where Soldier 30 stood guard. Meanwhile, the Green Beret should head back up the slope, and then toward Gun 29.

From this point on, things happen very quickly. Keep an eye on Soldier 31: when he reaches the far end of the bridge, have the Green Beret shoot the barrel next to 29, destroying the gun. The Green Beret can run south and use the pick to descend the cliff face. Soldier 30 will run back as fast as he can. Have the Sniper pull out his pistol and open fire on 30 as he runs past the wall. Then run up to the machine gun at 32 and take out the gunner with the pistol, as well. Hey, the alarms are going off already. Who'll notice a few gunshots?

Figure 5-7.
Clear out the area around the bridge so you can escape once the supply base is burning.

Now one of your Commandos can go over by the barbed wire and shoot the barrel next to the water tower. Before firing, zoom out the view so you can witness the chain in all its glory. Better, save the mission at this point so you can show your friends your handiwork later on. When everything is burning, a jeep arrives at the bridge to pick you up. Get both Commandos aboard and away before enemy reinforcements can reach you.

MISSION 9: A COURTESY CALL

NORTH AFRICA, OCTOBER 20, 1942

In El Alamein, a single question weighs on everyone's mind: Why doesn't Montgomery order the attack? Meanwhile, the British general builds up an overwhelming superiority in men and equipment before starting the offensive.

To disconcert Rommel's troops before the attack, you'll travel across the line of minefields in Bab el Qattara to the camp of the 21st Panzer Division. There you'll await dawn. Destroy as many objectives as you can, and then disappear.

MISSION SUMMARY

Objective: Destroy the communications control building, the antenna, the weapons store, the command post, and the bunker.

Team: Green Beret, Sniper, Sapper, Driver, Spy

After the last mission, this one is a welcome relief. It's quick, on a small map with few guards. You also have five Commandos, so each can exercise his specialty. Begin by infiltrating the base; then clear it of guards and blow up the objectives. The Sapper carries only two explosives, but explosive barrels are available in the base. Three tanks parked in the northwest corner of the base pose a major threat. You must eliminate them.

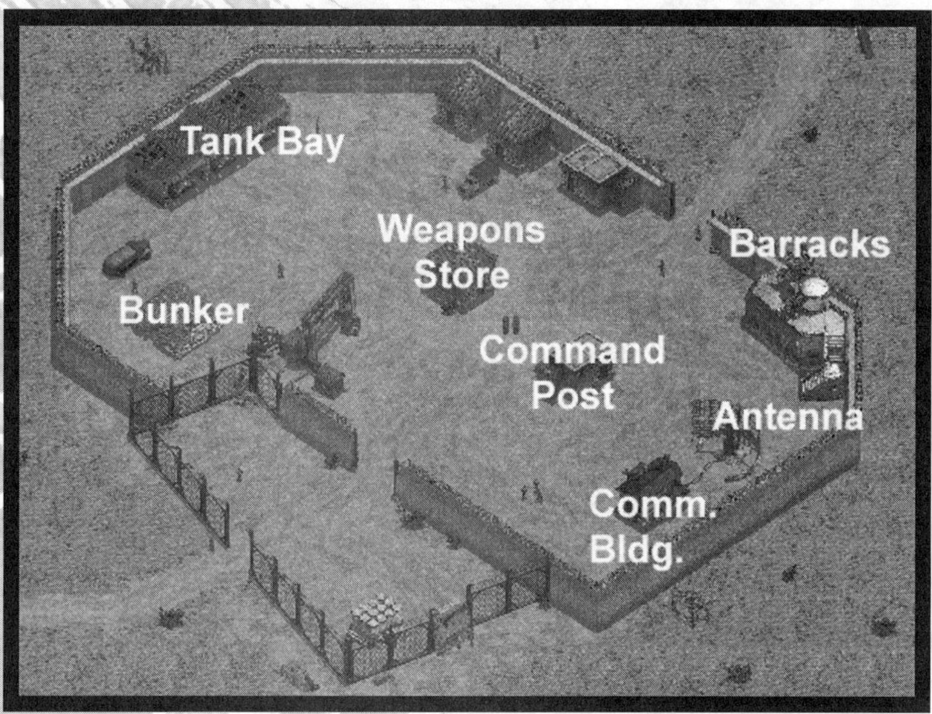

Figure 5-8. A Courtesy Call

PHASE 1: INFILTRATE AND SECURE THE BASE

A short mission where you get to blow up a lot of buildings—what more could you ask for? The Green Beret, Sniper, and Sapper begin in the south, the Driver and Spy in the north. As if the small number of guards weren't enough, your Spy saved his German officer's uniform from his last mission. No robbing the laundry this time around.

Get the Spy moving right at the start. Walk through the east gate, across the yard, and out the west gate. Move next to Soldier 1 and keep an eye on 2. When he walks past you going north, quickly take out 1 with the lethal injection and carry the body behind the containers to the south. Next, kill Soldier 2 at the south end of his route, just as he turns north. Again, move the body behind the containers. Finally, just walk over to Soldier 3 and poison him, careful to move the body out of sight.

Figure 5-9. The Spy can make short work of the three guards at the western gate.

Figure 5-10. There are only four guards in the north part of the base.

Have the Spy walk over toward the bunker and stand right behind Soldier 4. When 5 and 8 aren't looking, kill 4 and move the body behind the bunker. Then walk over to where Soldier 5 turns around near the bunker. When 8 isn't looking, kill 5 and carry the body out of sight. Now walk over to the eastern gate.

Standing right behind Soldier 6, wait until 7 passes you heading north and Patrol 10 is moving away. Then take out 6 and move his body through the gate and a little east and out of sight. Next, kill Soldier 7 and remove his body. Take a break from killing for a bit, walk over to Patrol 10, and strike up a conversation. Make sure they're looking away from the west gate. Now bring in the three Commandos waiting in the south. They must run quickly to the weapons store and hide inside. Now walk the Spy over to Soldier 9 and distract him while the Green Beret sneaks out of the weapons store and knifes Soldier 8. (Make sure Patrol 10 isn't looking.) Hide the body in a barrel and then kill 9. Hide the body behind a building and then hide the Green Beret, as well.

Time for another conversation with the patrol. The Spy must keep them looking southwest so all the objectives are out of their view. Now for the fun part: Bring the Driver onto the base and into the fuel truck. Drive to and park in front of the tank bay. Then run into one of the buildings by the other truck. The Sapper must place his explosives next to the bunker and the barracks. Taking out the latter

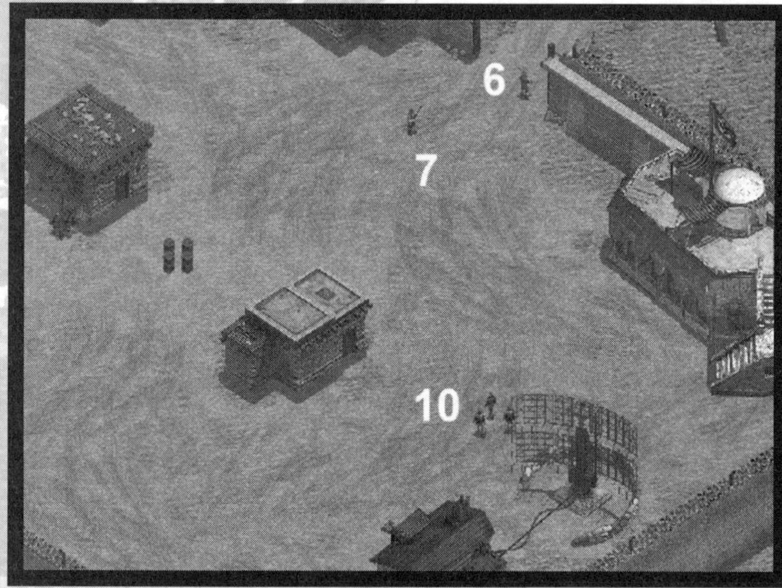

Figure 5-11. The Spy must clear the guards from around the base's east gate.

Figure 5-12. The Driver parks the fuel truck next to the tanks. When the explosives go off, they'll blow up the fuel truck and destroy all three tanks.

prevents reinforcements from pouring into the base. When the explosives go off, the two patrols outside the base walls will run in. Therefore, place the trap in the middle of the eastern gate. You'll at least take out one of the patrol soldiers. The Green Beret has the heavy work. He must move barrels next to the east and west warehouses, the antenna (within the sand bags), and the communications control building (at the west corner). Hide the Green Beret and Driver in one of the buildings near the truck. The Sniper and Sapper should go prone behind those buildings. You're ready for the next phase.

PHASE 2: FIREWORKS

Everything's ready, so let the show begin. The Spy can break off his conversation with the patrol and move toward the south corner of the base. When the patrol isn't looking and walks by the communications control building, whip out the pistol and shoot the barrel. Quickly put the pistol away and switch to the Sapper. Detonate both explosives by pressing [A] twice; then run into a building to hide.

Have the Sniper crawl to where he has a good shot at the east gate. Stay prone. When the first patrol walks through the gate, the trap will kill one soldier. Only five more to go. And the Sniper just happens to have five bullets. Drop the other two soldiers in the patrol, go prone again, and wait for the other patrol. Zoom out the map to see which gate they're approaching. If they're headed for the east gate, stay put. Otherwise, move the Sniper so he has a good view of the west gate. Take out the last patrol and you're almost done.

The Spy, while waiting for the patrols, can shoot the other barrels if he has time, but don't let anyone see him do it. Once all the objective buildings are burning and the area is clear of enemies, load all your Commandos into the truck and drive out the west gate, along the road, and off the map to safety.

NOTE

When the barracks explodes, a soldier or two may run out. You can kill them with the Spy, but don't waste the Sniper's precious ammunition on them. These Germans are in shock and will only run out the east gate and off the map.

MISSION 10: OPERATION ICARUS

NORTH AFRICA, NOVEMBER 14, 1942

Ten days have passed since the battle of El Alamein, which brought a dramatic change of roles in North Africa. Rommel's troops have retreated to the Libyan city of Agheila after a long, hard-fought withdrawal.

Captain George McRae of the Royal Air Force was shot down during a reconnaissance flight over German positions and taken prisoner near the El Agheila airfield. You must infiltrate the camp and rescue him.

MISSION SUMMARY

Objective: Rescue the downed pilot, destroy the weapons store, and blow up the two Ju-87 Stuka dive-bombers.

Team: Green Beret, Sniper, Sapper, Driver

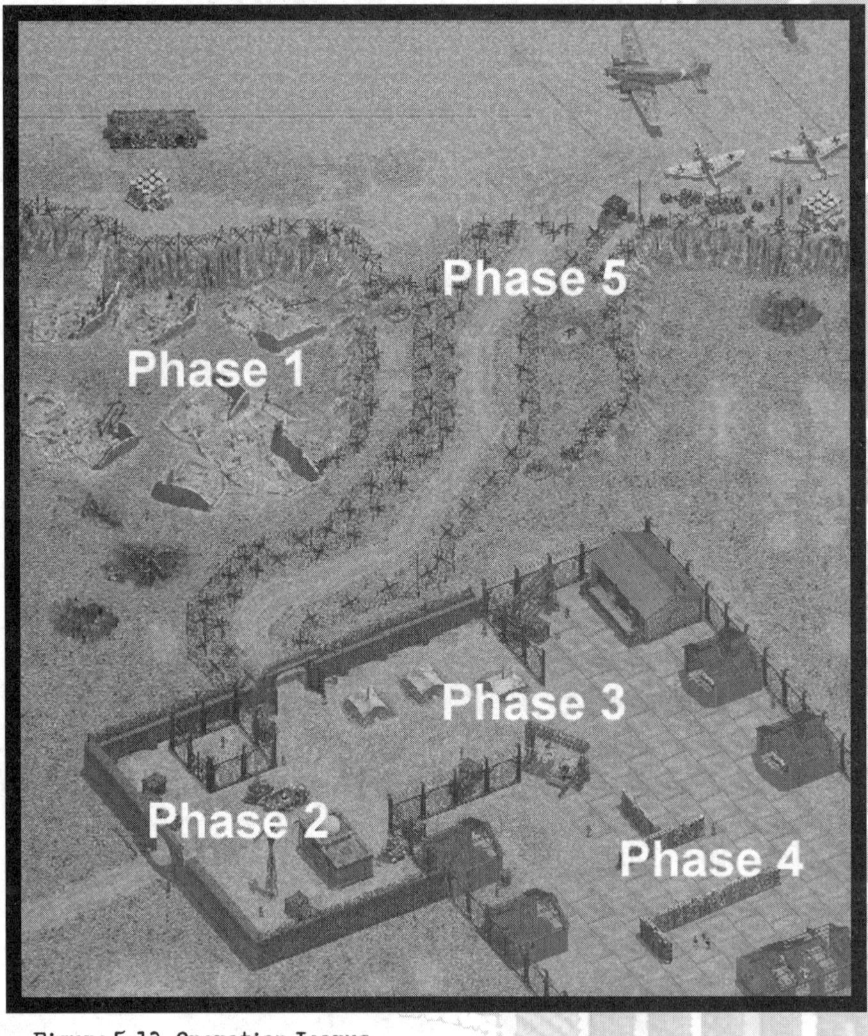

Figure 5-13. Operation Icarus

This basic rescue mission includes orders to demolish some targets while you're in the area. It looks very tough, but it won't be so bad if you tackle the mission methodically. The Spy would make this mission a lot easier, but you can accomplish

it without him. Your Commandos begin in the west-central part of the map. They must clear the area first, and then make their way into the base. Inside, the team must release the prisoner and clear the interior of guards. You must remain silent and out of sight: an alarm will summon not only all the soldiers in the barracks, but four tanks (and a failed mission), as well. Commandeer the vacant tank, however, and you'll have a chance. Before leaving the base, blow up the weapons store and head for the transport waiting on the runway. Destroy the two dive-bombers on your way, and then head for home.

PHASE 1: OUTSIDE THE BASE

Your four Commandos begin behind a wall in the midst of ruins. Several guards patrol all around. You'll need perfect timing to make it through without losing a team member. When no one's looking, the Green Beret and Sapper must crawl around and hide behind the wall immediately east of the start position. Wait until Patrol 4 heads south and soldiers 2 and 3 begin walking away. Then the Green Beret must pop up, run to 1, kill him, and quickly run after and kill 2. When Soldier 3 heads south again, take him out, too. Hide the Green Beret behind the walls south of 3.

Patrol 4 will make its way back toward the action. In fact, the soldiers may spot the Green Beret and come after him. Run him back to where the Sapper is hiding. When the patrol comes in range, the Sapper should lob a grenade and take them

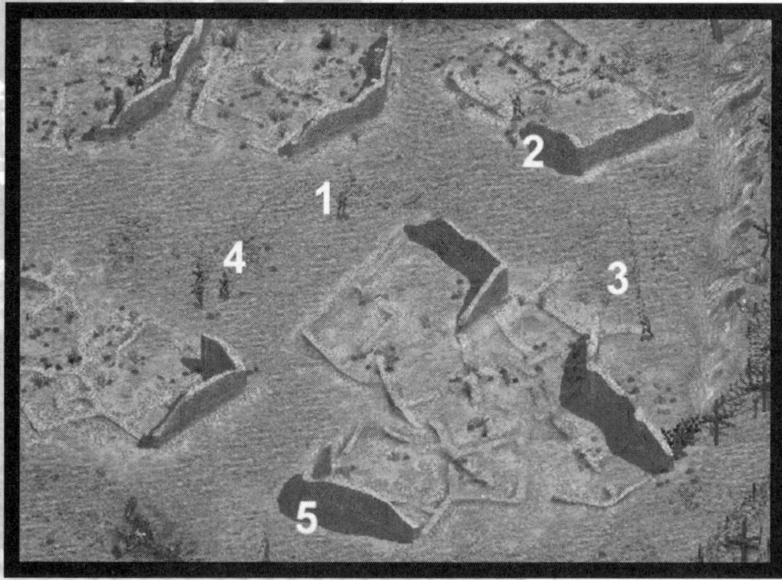

Figure 5-14.
You must eliminate all German soldiers patrolling outside before you can enter the base.

NOTE
You can also use firearms freely in this phase.

all out. Soldier 5 will respond to the explosion. Keep all of your Commandos prone and when 5 heads away, the Green Beret can knife him. With the area clear, you can run all your Commandos down toward the base. Hide them on the north side of the wall's west corner.

PHASE 2: INFILTRATING THE BASE

This part of the mission is difficult and requires some quick actions. Soldier 6 patrols outside the gate. When he begins heading south, send the Green Beret running after

Figure 5-15. Getting into the base is tough, but the Green Beret will clear the way on his own.

him—but don't knife him until he passes the gate. Next, place the decoy toward the south corner of the wall, near where Soldier 8 ends his patrol. Run back north to the other side of the gate and climb the wall with the pick. Scale down the other side and hide behind the boxes.

When 8 nears the decoy, activate it; then knife Soldier 7 when he walks south. Quickly run south and take out 8 while he's still distracted. Hide the body near the weapons store so Soldier 9 won't see it, and then knife 9 when he turns and heads east. Move the body back by 8's. Finally, sneak up behind Soldier 10, give him the blade, and move the body. You'll need the decoy later, so retrieve it now.

Bring all your Commandos into the base and hide them in the weapons store.

PHASE 3: THE NORTHERN SECTOR

This phase is fairly easy if you do it right. You must clear all the enemy soldiers out of the northern sector of the base. Normally you'd take out 12 or 13 first. However, Soldier 11 in the corner has a good view of both of them.

The Sniper is the solution: bring him out and crawl to a position where he can drop 11. Quickly drop to the prone position again and return to the weapons store. Now the Green Beret can sneak up and knife 12, and then 13. Move the bodies out of sight; then crawl over to where 11 lies lifeless. When Patrol 20 (see figure 5-17)

Figure 5-16. This phase is short and to the point. Your team must kill only four soldiers.

heads south, and Soldier 14 is moving north, run after 14 and knife him. Leave the body and drop prone.

After killing the guards in this area, send a Commando to the detention pen and let the pilot out. Then return both to hide in the weapons store.

PHASE 4: COMMANDEER A TANK

Position the Green Beret over by the shed at 24. Wait until Patrol 20 heads away, and then approach Soldier 15. You must time this exactly, so 15 won't cry out before you can kill him. Carry the body to the other side of 24; then crawl over behind the tank under repair. Place the decoy there, and then hide behind the boxes to the west. Activate the decoy and Soldier 16 will come over to have a look. As he walks away, run and stab him with your knife. Move the body behind cover. Recover the decoy and crawl over behind 17 after Patrol 20 heads south again. Move the body out of sight, and then crawl over by the disassembled tank.

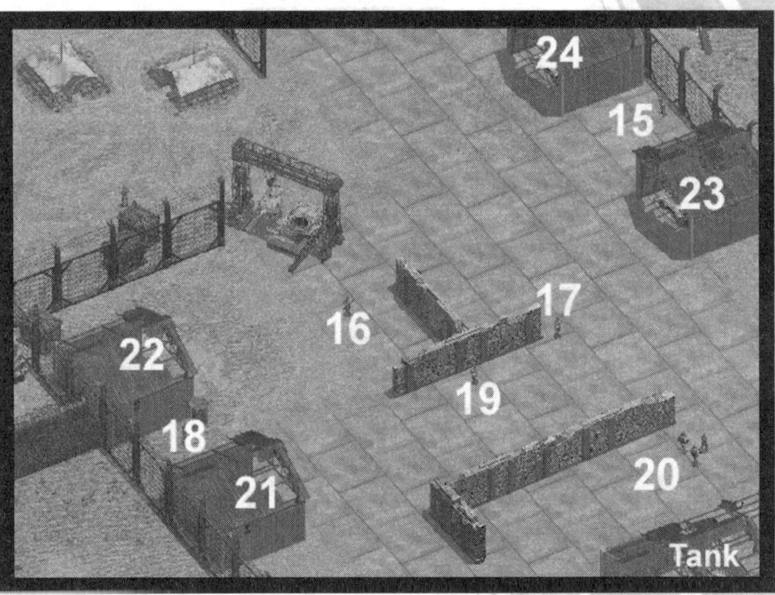

Figure 5-17. The tank's in the southeast, but to get to it, you must kill a few more soldiers.

While the Green Beret gets the job done, the Sniper must move into position for another two kills—out the west gate and around, so he's directly behind Soldier 18. Keep down on the ground or 19 will see you. Wait until Patrol 20 heads south and has just passed 19. Then, when 19 turns east, quickly take out 18 and 19 with the precision rifle. Have the Sniper run back and hide in the weapons store, because he's out of bullets now. Before Patrol 20 can find Body 19, the Green Beret must move it around to the west side of the wall, out of sight.

Move all Commandos into the weapons store, except the Sapper and the Driver. Run them over to the wall near 16's post. Move the Sapper between 21 and 22 while the Driver heads toward the wall west of 21. Save the mission here: the next part moves very quickly.

When Patrol 20 heads away from the Driver's position, send him running to the tank. When he hops in, the alarm will go off. Because there's no longer any need for subtlety, the Sapper can throw a grenade at Tank 21 and then another quickly at 22. Before the enemy can get the Sapper, move him over to where the Driver's been hiding. With the Driver in the tank, move it forward a bit. Take out Patrol 20, and then wait to see what Tank 23 will do. Tank 24 will head out the north gate toward the airfield. Because only other tanks can take out your tank, keep a close eye on them. For safety, the Sapper should climb aboard the tank as well. When Tank 23 heads away from you, the Driver must dart out from behind the wall and blow it up with the main gun.

TIP

Ctrl-click to fire either of a tank's two weapons. The machine gun shoots at nearby targets, but the main gun requires a greater range. To take out enemy tanks, then, don't get too close, or you won't destroy them.

Soldiers will pour out of the barracks in the northeast corner of the base. Move over and keep killing them until the building is empty. Next, move over to the weapons store and pick up the other Commandos. When the building is empty, send the Sapper to place the time bomb next to it. Then reboard the tank.

Figure 5-18. The Driver, who is in a captured tank, blasts Tank 23 in a duel. The turret must move before it can fire, so make sure the enemy's turret is turned away from you before you approach.

PHASE 5: ON TO THE AIRFIELD

With all the Commandos (and the rescued pilot) onboard, head the tank out the north gate. Wait until Tank 24 heads toward the airfield, but before it passes through the gate. You must take out this tank before it fires at you. Ignore the machine-gun nests until the other tank is in flames. Then destroy all three machine-gun nests along the road. Move to the end of the road and fire on the reinforcements coming out of the barracks. Try to take out the Stuka dive-bombers, as well. If you can't hit them, you can use the nearby explosive barrels later.

After you kill all the reinforcements (when no more come out), get everyone out of the tank and run over to the waiting Ju-52 transport. The pilot will start the engines and take off. Mission accomplished.

MISSION 11: INTO THE SOUP

NORTH AFRICA. DECEMBER 3, 1942

Axis forces have commenced a strong counteroffensive from Tunisia. Meanwhile, the Allies will make small incursions in the Libyan zones under enemy control. Objectives: To cut supplies and communications and gather information about the strength of Rommel's forces.

Your mission is to cross enemy lines to the oil fields at Maradeh, south of El Agheila, and destroy the drilling rigs to divert south some divisions of the Afrika Korps.

MISSION SUMMARY

Objective: To destroy all four oil rigs on the map.

Team: Green Beret, Sniper, Sapper, Driver, Spy

Figure 5-19. Into the Soup

This is another large mission, but the hardest part takes place at the beginning. Your Commandos start in the middle of the western map edge. They must clear the German camp of opposition, and then infiltrate the drilling sites. All team members must work together to complete the mission. Capturing the vacant half-track provides a means of escape, but its machine gun also helps you accomplish your objectives. You must destroy all four oil rigs before you leave the map.

PHASE 1: THE CAMP

Your work's cut out for you: this is the mission's most difficult phase. But don't be discouraged. The Spy was kind enough to bring along his German officer's uniform. Without it, this mission would be impossible.

Send him down to distract Soldier 4 so the Green Beret can sneak up on 1 and knife him. Watch for Soldier 3 and Patrol 13, both now and during the steps that follow. Hide the body behind the small building. Repeat on Soldier 2, and then on 3 when his back is turned. Finally, give Soldier 4 the blade as the Spy talks to him. Carry each body behind the building.

Figure 5-20. The German camp is crawling with enemies. Once you clear them out, the rest of the mission is a breeze.

That conversation is dead, so send the Spy to distract Patrol 13 so they face south. This allows the Green Beret to kill Soldier 5. After dumping his body behind the building, watch 6. As he moves south, the Green Beret should make tracks in the sand in his field of view and then use the shovel to hide. Soldier 6 will see the tracks and come to investigate. Wait until his back is turned or he heads away before popping up and taking him down. As usual, hide the body.

The Spy should break away from the patrol and go talk to Soldier 7, keeping him faced south and away from the Green Beret as he approaches for the kill. The body can stay behind the tent, because no one can see it there. Next, have the Spy distract Soldier 8 at the south end of his route. Keep him looking north and the Green Beret will have little trouble taking him out. When no one's looking, dump the body back by 7's. Now send the Spy to divert Soldier 10's attention to the south. This gives the Green Beret the opportunity to sneak up on 9 and knife him.. Now send the Spy to distract Soldier 11 so the Green Beret can kill 10. Soldier 12 is next on the Spy's list. This time the Green Beret should follow Patrol 13 on the south leg of their walk, take out Soldier 11, and move his body over by 7's, behind the tent. On Patrol 13's next lap, the Green Beret can kill Soldier 12 and remove the body.

Now things get tricky: the Spy must divert Patrol 13's attention from the Green Beret. He must carry a barrel of explosives and place it next to the west part of the barracks displaying the German flag. Then position him so he can follow the patrol as it moves south. When they move near the barrel, whip out the pistol and watch both barracks and patrol go up in flames.

Quickly hide the Green Beret in the sand, because reinforcements from the east will come to investigate. The Spy can play dumb, but he must keep Patrol 14 in the area using his Distract skill. After the other soldiers return to their posts, the Green Beret can come up out of the sand, grab another explosive barrel, and move it over by Patrol 14. Before detonating it, bring the rest of the team forward. Position the Sapper behind the building adjacent to the barracks. The Driver can hide by Soldier 7's tent while the Sniper moves over by the water tower. The rest occurs in Phase 2.

PHASE 2: ACCESS TO THE DRILLING SITES

The Sniper's post for this phase is the little building you see in figure 5-21. However, Soldier 15, up on the ridge, watches over it. Carefully crawl along the road toward 15 until he's in range and drop him with the precision rifle. Then quickly hide in the building. The Sapper can set a trap along the ridge east of the water tower and eliminate one more soldier. Everything's ready, so the Green Beret can blow the barrel and take out Patrol 14. Make sure that the Spy is far enough away to avoid injury. The Green Beret should hide under the sand and wait, along with the

Figure 5-21. Your team must eliminate these guards to reach the drilling rigs.

other Commandos, for the other German soldiers to come and see what all the noise was about.

Usually four soldiers will make their way to you—16, 18, 19, and 27. One will walk into the trap. The other three walk around near the water tower before leaving. The Sapper must throw the grenade before they leave. Try to get all three at once. If you can't, then take out at least two. The Green Beret or Spy can take out the last one.

The explosions took place far enough from the barracks in the middle of the map that the alarm there didn't sound. It's time to continue the advance: move the Spy into the lead while the rest of the team joins the Sniper in the little building. The Spy must distract Soldier 17 at the gate so he faces north. Then the Green Beret can cut his throat and haul the body out of sight.

PHASE 3: SECURE THE HALF-TRACK

The Spy must run around through the center of the map and then east to find Soldier 21. You must stop 21 out of Soldier 23's line of sight. Divert 21's attention from

Figure 5-22. Several soldiers, including a machine-gun nest, guard the vacant half-track. But the Spy and Green Beret will clear out all the enemies easily.

Soldier 20. The Green Beret can use the pick to scale the ridge south of 20 and then crawl over to kill him with the knife. Move the body over by 15's. Then climb down the ladder, kill 21, and move the body behind the rock.

Now the Spy must distract 23 while the Green Beret knifes machine-gunner 22 and removes the body. Have the Green Beret crawl along the eastern map edge and then west so he's directly behind 23. While the Spy distracts 24 outside the gate, take out 23 and move the body.

After this is done, the Green Beret should crawl over to the corner of the wall and ridge, west of the building. Make a lot of footprints in the sand and then dig a hole to hide in. The Spy should break off the conversation and walk back through the gate. Soldier 24 will see the footprints and come to investigate. Use the Spy to divert 24's attention from the Green Beret's hiding place so he can pop up and silently kill 24. Move the body into the corner and take a quick break before going on to the next phase.

PHASE 4: WIPE OUT THE MAIN GARRISON

This could be a very difficult phase, but you've already made it a little easier by killing four of the soldiers in the previous two phases. Send the Spy to distract Patrol 28 so they look west. Then move your Sniper through the gate, crawling, so he has a shot at both 25 and 26 on the roof of the barracks. Make sure

Figure 5-23. The center of the map contains a lot of troops, but you whittled their numbers down during phases 2 and 3.

Soldier 29 is moving south, and then shoot 25, quickly followed by 26. Although no one can see their dead bodies on the roof, if another soldier sees them shot, an alarm will sound.

The Sniper can now take cover in a building, along with the Sapper, while the Driver heads for the vacant half-track. Hop aboard and drive it through the gate. The Spy should run for cover as the Driver mows down Patrol 28, Soldier 29, and any Germans coming out of the barracks. The half-track is armored, but enough enemy fire can destroy it.

PHASE 5: BLOW THE RIGS!

The half-track you commandeered makes this phase a snap, as well. But you must prepare before you go barreling out the gate: send the Spy to distract Patrol 30 while the Sapper places explosives next to the two southern oil rigs. Then move the Sapper to place the last explosive in the tunnel. Move all your team (except the Sapper) into the half-track, where they'll be safe from small arms fire. Be sure the half-track

Figure 5-24.
The Sapper can detonate an explosive in the tunnel to cut off reinforcements from the north—including the other half-track.

TIP

To destroy the northern half-track, don't detonate the explosive in the tunnel until the alarm sounds in the north. Wait until you can see the half-track just about to exit the tunnel, and then order the Sapper to blow the charges. The tunnel will come crashing down *and* you'll take out the half-track.

and all your Commandos are a safe distance from the explosives. Detonate all three by pressing [A] three times.

Get the Sapper on the half-track and drive out the west gate. Follow the road around to the north. Take out Patrol 30 and continue east to take out 31. As you drive the half-track along the ridge to the east, you'll be able to fire at the reinforcements coming out of the barracks to the north.

The final two oil rigs are your main concern, however. Wait until a fuel truck drives between the two rigs and then blast it with the machine guns. The truck will blow up, taking the rigs with it. Finally, back up along the ridge and follow the road west to safety.

Figure 5-25. The half-track can drive along the ridge. By shooting at the fuel truck when it's between the two oil rigs, you can destroy them all at once.

MISSION 12: UP ON THE ROOF

NORTH AFRICA, MARCH 15, 1943

The Allied armies have gained control of Libya. Their next step is to expel the enemy from Tunisia, but they encounter fierce resistance in the form of the Mareth Line.

In the course of a covert operation to gather information from Axis defenses, your men have been caught up in a sweep by German soldiers. They got away and are scattered around the city. A small rescue operation is underway.

MISSION SUMMARY

Objective: To release the Informer from confinement and then get him and all the Commandos to the Kubelwagen, which will drive them to safety.

Team: Green Beret, Sniper, Spy, Informer

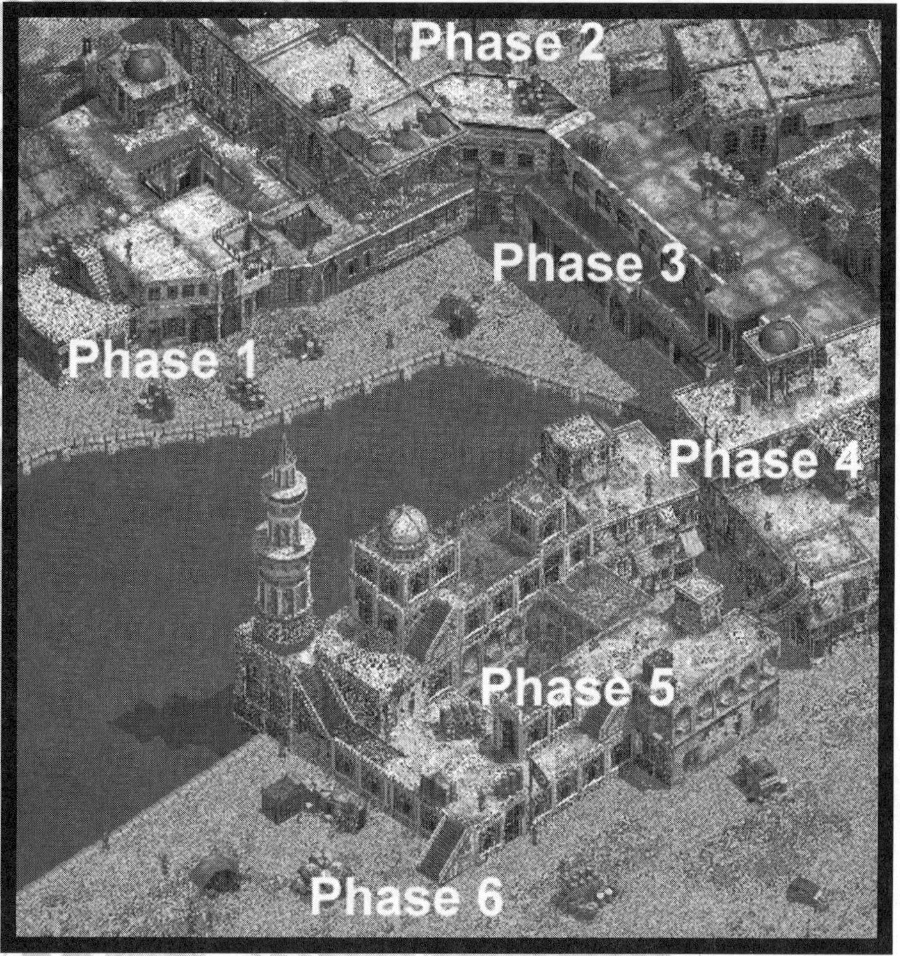

Figure 5-26.
Up on the Roof

The city is swarming with German soldiers looking for your men. As if that weren't enough, your three Commandos are separated. First, you must make your way to the rooftops in the north and clear them of all opposition. This done, you must release the Informer. Finally, you must eliminate all the soldiers in the south so your team can escape. This mission requires clever strategy—and skill—at killing the enemy quickly and efficiently.

PHASE 1: GET TO THE ROOFTOPS

The Spy begins in the courtyard. The Green Beret hides at ground level in a building to the west. This phase's goal is to get the Green Beret up to the rooftops where he can get to work. The Spy must distract the patrol in the courtyard so the Green Beret can sneak out of the building. Wait until Soldier 1 walks past going west, then run, kill him, and quickly carry the body around the corner. During this, watch out for Soldier 3, on the roof.

With the Green Beret hiding behind the corner of the row of buildings, the Spy can finish his conversation with the patrol and make his way over to the ladder in the west. Climb it and wait for Soldier 2. When 3 and 4 look the other way, give 2 a lethal injection and then carry the body to the door in the stairs and drop it there. Next, the Spy climbs the stairs and distracts Soldier 5 on the balcony so the Green Beret can kill 3 when 4 moves away, and move the body down the stairs.

Figure 5-27. The Green Beret, hiding at ground level in a building, must make his way to the rooftops with the Spy's help.

TIP

With all the soldiers in this mission, it's easy to be caught in the act of killing by a soldier you didn't think could see you. We recommend saving the mission at least once per phase and quicksaving after every kill, unless you must kill several enemies in rapid succession. Some of the steps in this mission are very difficult, and you won't want to have to repeat them after you've already succeeded.

Now move the Spy over to distract Soldier 14 (see figure 5-28). To get there, he must climb the ladder by 13, and then walk across to the ladder behind 14. Good timing is crucial for this kill. Both the patrol *and* Soldier 5 must be walking away from 4. When the coast is clear, have the Green Beret knife 4, and then quickly drop to the prone position and crawl back down the stairs. Leave the body where it lies. No one can see it.

When the patrol moves southeast, run after Soldier 5 when he heads away and give him the blade. Quickly move the body into the corner of the balcony and out of sight. Finally, the Green Beret must crawl over to the ladder near 13 and wait for the next phase.

PHASE 2: CLEARING OUT THE NORTHERN ROOFTOPS

Phase 2 is this mission's most difficult. It requires impeccable timing and teamwork. Get the Spy up the ladder and over to Soldier 13. Divert his attention from the nearby ladder, as well as the house, so the Green Beret can climb up and then crawl over there to hide. Keep an eye on 6 and 7: they can spot the Green Beret at his most vulnerable moments—when he stands after climbing the ladder and when he enters the house. Once you get the Green Beret into the house, the Spy must divert Soldier 12's attention from the ladder.

It's time for the Sniper to leave the house. Again, make sure the coast is clear, and then crawl west and hide under the ledge. From there, make sure you can target Soldier 6 when he's near the crates and Soldier 7 at the west end of his walk. When you're in position, take out 6 when 7 walks west, and then drop 7, as well.

Figure 5-28. The northern area is full of soldiers close enough together to watch over each other.

Hit [C] to quickly drop prone again. Soldier 8 will see 6's body and come to take a look. When he's behind the crates, take him out, as well.

Now crawl over toward the edge of the roof east of 13. Find a single position where the Sniper can target soldiers 9, 10, and 11. You must take out all three without any of them sounding an alarm. Wait until 10 walks over to 9 and turns around. Then, as quickly as possible, shoot 9 and 10, and then 11. One of the guards may see the others die. Just shoot him before he can sound the alarm. If the alarm does go off, begin at your last quicksave and try again. While the Spy is still talking to Soldier 13, the Green Beret can knife him. Send the Spy to poison 12, and the phase is complete.

PHASE 3: RELEASE THE PRISONER

Now the Spy must make his way back down the ladder by 13 and distract Soldier 16 toward the west. Then, when the patrol is moving west, send the Green Beret down the ladder behind 14 and knife him. Crawl over and repeat the process on 15 and climb back up to the roof. The Green Beret must make his way over to 16 and kill him, careful to move the body out of sight and always keeping an eye on the patrol down in the courtyard. With 16 dead, the Spy must climb down to the courtyard and distract the patrol east of the jail so they face south or west. This allows the Green Beret to release the Informer and get both back up on the roof. Then the Spy can end his conversation with the patrol and join his teammates.

PHASE 4: THE SOUTHEAST SECTOR

While the Sniper and Informer stay near the house by 13, the Spy and Green Beret can make their way east. The Spy must distract Soldier 18 toward the west so the Green Beret can plant the decoy north of the building near 17. Hide the Green Beret near 12 and activate the decoy. Have the Spy follow 17 and poison him when 18 isn't looking. When he spots the body, he'll come over, along with 19. As long as the Spy was not seen poisoning 17, his cover is secure. Poison both 18 and 19, doing in each when the other isn't looking. If one cries out and sets off an alarm, don't worry: it will sound only in the courtyard below. The reinforcements who come out of the barracks down there won't compromise the mission's success.

Send the Spy to distract Soldier 23 near the stairs, facing south. Then the Green Beret can kill Soldier 20 when 21 walks away and hide the body behind the building. Wait until 21 comes back; after he turns around, run after him with the knife.

Figure 5-29. The Spy and the Green Beret must work together to clear this area of soldiers.

Take him out quickly, followed by 22. Leave the bodies while the Green Beret sneaks behind 23 and kills him.

Drop the Green Beret prone so the other soldiers in the area won't spot him, and bring the Sniper and Informer to hide behind the building near 17.

PHASE 5: CLEARING OUT THE MOSQUE

The success of this whole phase hinges on the Spy's skills. He begins by walking over to Soldier 24 and quietly poisoning him. Then make your way over to 25 and kill him. You want to be seen by 26; however, after he cries out, go prone and put the uniform back on. If he sounds the alarm, you'll have to try this step again. Otherwise, 26 will come to investigate and 27 and 28 will usually join him. Kill each individually when the others aren't looking.

Killing four soldiers in this spot clears out a good portion of the southern area, making the rest of the mission easier. Now walk behind 29 and kill him when no one's looking. Soldier 30 is your next target. Poison him when 33 looks away. Now

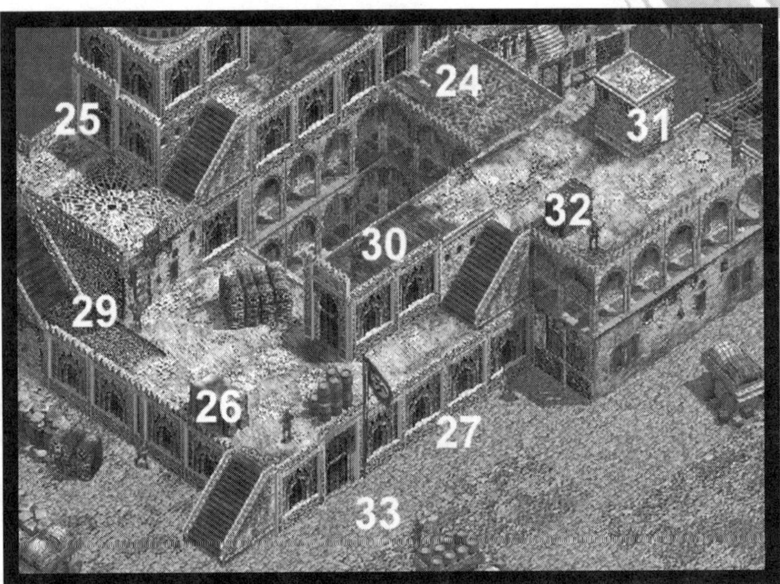

Figure 5-30. The Mosque must be cleared of enemy soldiers before your Commandos can escape.

the Spy can walk over and kill 31 and 32, but make sure no one's watching, especially the patrol below.

PHASE 6: THE GETAWAY

The mission is almost complete. The Spy makes his way down to stand by Soldier 33. When the patrol passes heading west, take out 33 and carry his body northeast to hide it in the alley. Walk over to Soldier 34 and kill him behind the crates after the patrol has passed by heading west. When they turn and go back east, kill 35 and hide his body by 34. Now run after the patrol and distract them so they face south. This gives the rest of the team—Green Beret, Sniper, and Informer—the chance to come running across the mosque and then down to the alley where 33's body is hidden. After they're in the alley, the Spy can dismiss the patrol and let them continue their march. As they head west, order all your Commandos to run for the Kubelwagen in the southeast corner. It will take them out of the city to safety.

Figure 5-31.
Once you kill the soldiers, hide their bodies next to the Mosque.

CHAPTER 6

THE EUROPEAN CAMPAIGN

The Allies have driven Axis forces from North Africa, and your successful missions contributed to this outcome. But the war isn't over yet. The Allies are planning their return to France. You must help prepare the way for the landings on the beaches of Normandy, and then the advance on Germany. This campaign's eight missions will require all the skills you learned in Norway and North Africa. Let's get started.

MISSION 13: DAVID AND GOLIATH

FRANCE, MAY 15, 1944

The Allies sank the battleship *Bismarck*, jewel of the *Kreigsmarine*, in May 1941, during her first sortie in the North Atlantic. This ship was powerful enough to sink the battle cruiser *Hood* and involve the entire Royal Navy in a long, painful chase.

Reports indicate that a replica of the *Bismarck* has been built in the port of Le Havre, and departs today to patrol the coast of Normandy. The French Resistance can help us put four men there. If we can sabotage that ship, we'll put an early end to the rebirth of a legend, and facilitate future operations in the zone.

MISSION SUMMARY

Objective: Sink the *Bismarck II* and destroy the fuel tanks.

Team: Green Beret, Sniper, Marine, Sapper, Driver

Your first mission in the European theater is explosive. It's not all that difficult, but a few steps are extremely challenging and will require all the skills you've learned so far.

Your team of five Commandos begins in the southeast. You really could use the Spy in this mission, but he's assigned elsewhere. The Commandos first must clear out the southern jetties, and then the docks in the center of the map. This will allow you to get your entire team into the base. Then you must eliminate all enemy soldiers without setting off the alarm. Once the base is clear, your team can prepare to destroy the objectives and formulate an escape plan. The escape is one of the mission's toughest aspects.

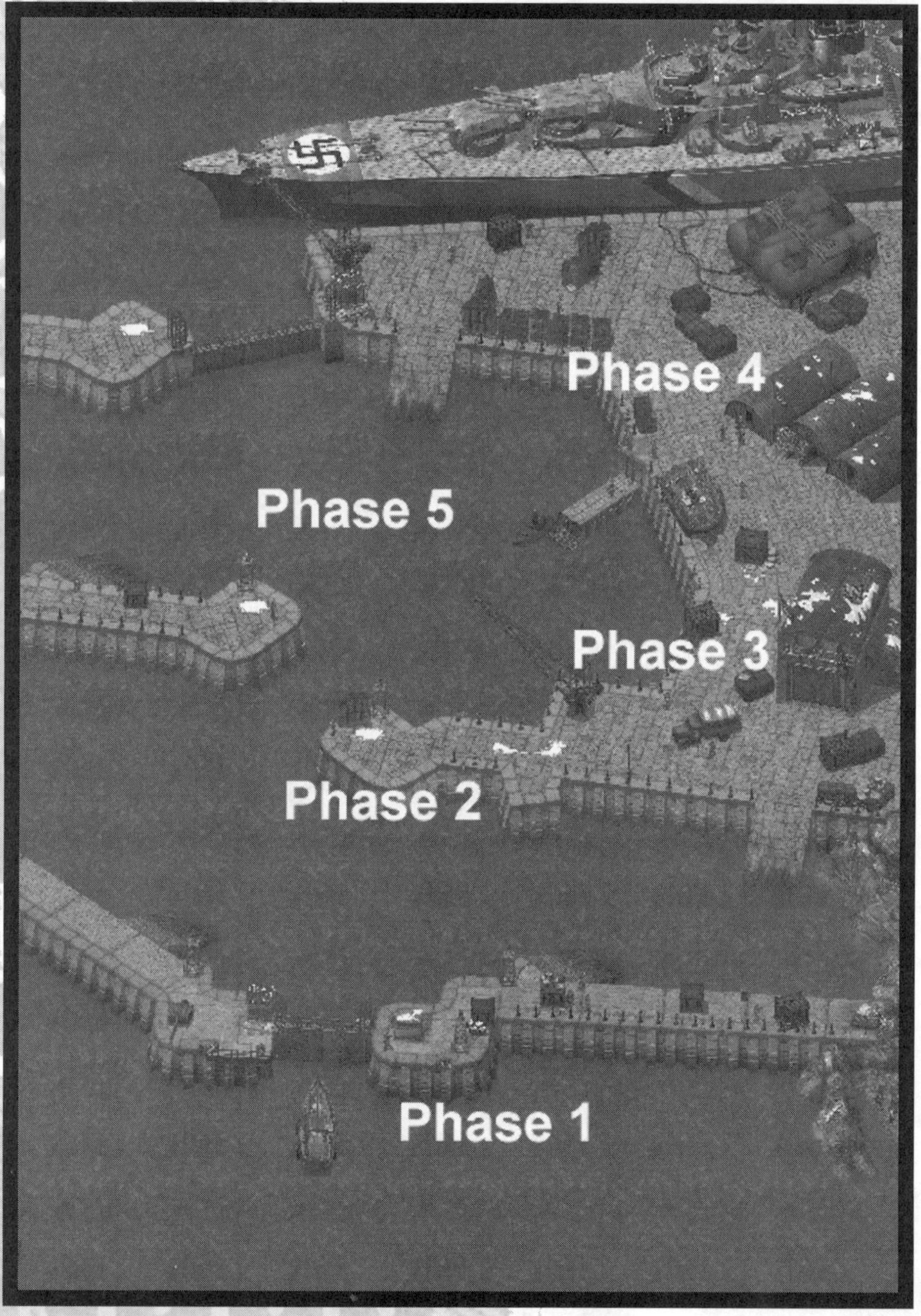

Figure 6-1. David and Goliath

PHASE 1: THE SOUTHERN JETTY

This is a fairly easy phase for someone with your experience. First, put the Marine in the water so he can swim to the gate. A boat approaches the gate and sounds a horn. Soldier 5 walks into the control shack, opens the gate, and closes it again after the boat passes through. The Marine must follow the boat into the base before the gate shuts.

While the Marine is waiting to enter, the Green Beret can pull out his trusty pick and climb the wall of the jetty in the east. Hide behind the large crate and wait for Soldier 2 to walk west. Then quickly knife 1, run after and kill 2, and then 3. Hide behind the crate near 3 until Soldier 4 approaches. When he turns around, take him out.

By now the Marine should be in the base. Swim to the ramp near Soldier 5. When he looks away, jump out of the water, run to 5 and kill him silently with either the knife or the speargun. Finally, walk into the control shack and open the gate.

Figure 6-2. Your team must clear this jetty and open the gates to get into the base.

PHASE 2: THE CENTRAL DOCKS

This phase isn't too difficult. With the gate open, your remaining Commandos can enter the base. First, however, the central docks must be cleared of soldiers. The Marine must re-enter the water and swim to the dock near soldiers 6 and 7. Watch the routes these two soldiers take as they patrol. When Soldier 7 heads west and 6 turns east, run toward 6. Follow him around and knife him when he gets between the two stacks of crates near the ramp. Wait for 7 to come back and then go after him when he heads west again.

This ramp is clear, so the Marine can swim to the ramp near the Green Beret and pull out the inflatable boat. Row the Green Beret across to the ramp the Marine just cleared and drop him off. Tie up the boat east of the ramp. In this phase, the Marine must be able to move quickly; the boat will just slow him down. Don the diving gear, and then swim to the ramp near Soldier 9 while the Green Beret crawls west along the dock until he's behind Soldier 8. Wait until 10 turns away, and then knife 8. The Green Beret can then crawl back and hide near the crates where 6's body lies.

Now it's the Marine's turn to kill. Soldier 9 occasionally walks over to the ramp, and then back to his post. When he turns around at the ramp, immediately pop up and take him out with the pistol—yes, the *pistol!* Drop back into the water quickly,

Figure 6-3.
Because the Marine can't carry bodies, you must take care to kill these two soldiers out of sight of other guards.

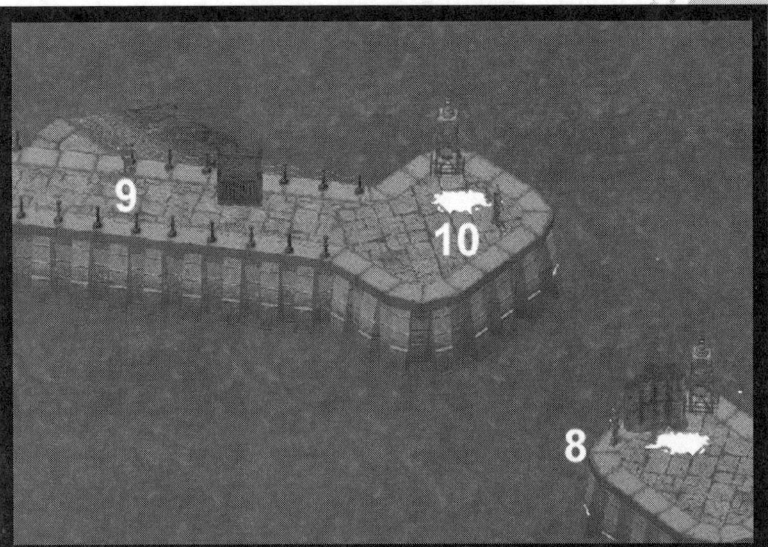

Figure 6-4.
The Green Beret and Marine must work together to take out these three soldiers without sounding an alarm.

because Soldier 10 hears the shots and comes running. He may walk near the ramp, where you can kill him with the speargun. But if he doesn't get that close, use the pistol on him when he turns his back.

Now return to the water and swim over to pick up the boat. Take it to pick up the Sniper, Sapper, and Driver, and then row them to the ramp where the Green Beret is waiting. Tie up the boat east of the ramp.

PHASE 3: ELIMINATING THE PATROL

You've reached one of the mission's most difficult parts, so save the game here. You'll probably have to replay this phase several times to get it right.

When Patrol 11 heads north, the Driver must move the truck so it's in front of the garage. Then make the Sniper crawl to the position shown on figure 6-5 and pull out the precision rifle. Hide the Green Beret behind the crate immediately west of the garage. Patrol 11 will come back and turn around between the crates. Keep your fingers on both [R] and [C]. When all the soldiers in the patrol are looking away, shoot one of the rear soldiers, quickly press [C] to drop prone after firing, and then

Figure 6-5.
The Sniper must kill all three soldiers in Patrol 11 without triggering an alarm.

press R to bring the precision rifle up again. Fire at the second soldier, repeat the two-key process, and then kill the third soldier.

Drop to the ground again and quickly crawl east. Practice the timing of this step so you can kill all of the soldiers before they see you, cry out, and set off the alarm. Soldier 12 will see the bodies of the patrol and go to investigate. When his back is turned, the Green Beret must take him out with the knife before he sounds the alarm. The alarm must not sound, or you'll have to restart at your last save.

TIP

Whenever the Sniper fires the precision rifle, he finishes in an upright position. It's a good practice to drop him prone after every shot to prevent surviving soldiers from spotting him. If you must kill a number of soldiers in sequence, drop after shooting one (C); then bring up the rifle again (R). After a little practice, you'll be able to do this without hesitation.

PHASE 4: KILL THE REST OF THE GUARDS

Put the Marine back in the water and swim to the ramp near Soldier 13. Make the Sniper crawl to the position shown in figure 6-6. Again, this step requires precise timing. Wait until Soldier 14 reaches the southern end of his walk and turns around. The Sniper then must shoot 13 and drop to the ground. Have the Marine jump out of the water quickly, run after 14, and kill him with the speargun. Move the Green Beret north and hide him south of the crates near 15. Wait until 15 turns north and then take him out with the blade. This clears the way for the Marine to sneak around the crate to a position behind Soldier 16, kill him, and then move over to take out 17, as well. Take this opportunity to open the northern gate at the control shack next to 13.

Only three more Germans to go. Walk down to stand behind Soldier 19. When he's not looking at 18, shoot 18 with the speargun, and then quickly knife 19. Climb down the ladder and, finally, kill Soldier 20.

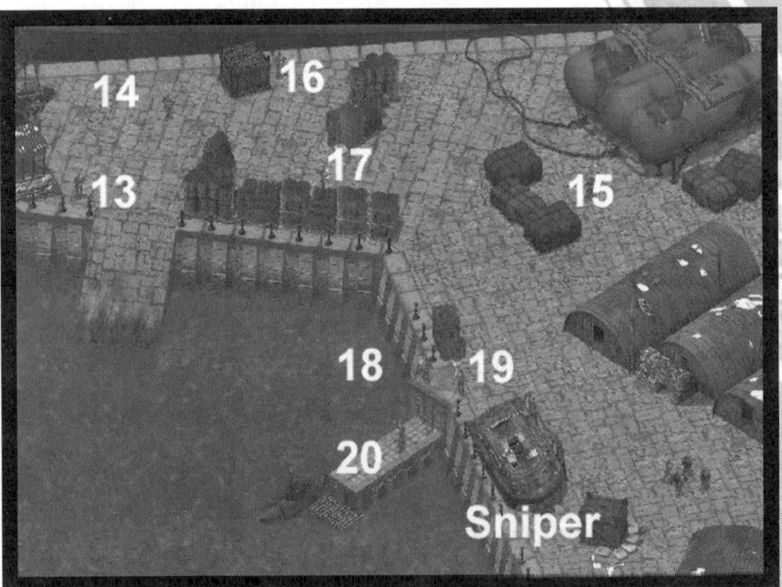

Figure 6-6. The remaining soldiers around the base are easy to kill.

PHASE 5: DESTRUCTION AND ESCAPE

It's time to get ready to destroy your mission objectives. The Sapper must place the explosives next to the fuel tanks in the northeast. The Driver must move the truck out onto the dock and position it carefully as shown in figure 6-7. The truck must be as far south and east as possible. In fact, save the game here so you can come back if the truck wasn't placed correctly. This blocks tank fire as your team escapes in the boat.

You're prepared, so load all your Commandos into the boat and row to the ramp near 5. Unload the Driver and send him to take control of the cannon. The Sapper must get out and the Marine should enter the water and swim to the pad near the submarine. Enter the sub and sail it toward the ramp near 9. Position it as close to the ramp as you can so you can still have a shot at the bow of the *Bismarck II.* The rest of the phase takes place very quickly, so save again here.

The Marine now can launch a torpedo at the battleship and then quickly sail the sub to the ramp. Get out of the sub and into the water. Swim to the boat and get it ready to go. The Sapper must detonate his explosive and then get into the boat. But don't leave just yet. A patrol boat will arrive near the buoy in the southwest. The Driver can sink it with the cannon, and then quickly run to the boat. As he's climbing aboard, the Marine must get the boat moving. Row out the gate toward the buoy. When you reach it, the mission ends.

Figure 6-7.
Placing the truck is critical.

If you positioned the truck improperly, the tank can fire its machine guns at your boat and kill some, if not all, of your Commandos. Even one death means failure, and you must play again. Just restart where you saved after moving the truck and try placing it again.

MISSION 14: D-DAY KICK OFF

FRANCE, MAY 25, 1944

Everything is ready for Operation Overlord. General Eisenhower only awaits good weather. At both sides of the English Channel, the tension mounts.

The latest aerial photographs show four powerful cannons placed near La Riviere, in the area code-named "Juno." These could pose a serious threat to the landings. Your mission: take them out. This is how you'll write the opening page of the greatest military landing in the history of war.

MISSION SUMMARY

Objective: Destroy all four coastal guns.

Team: Green Beret, Sniper, Marine, Sapper, Driver

This is a large mission involving more than fifty German soldiers, not counting reinforcements. Your team of Commandos must clear a landing area in the southwest. Once all are ashore, you can clear out the area near each of the first three gun emplacements. To reach the fourth emplacement, you must use stealth and cunning to commandeer the tank and use it to clear out the rest of the map.

Several steps during this mission demand precise timing. Many enemy soldiers are in view of three or four others at some point during their patrol. To complete this mission, you also must use all your Commandos as a team. The alarm must not sound until Phase 4, so stay quiet except when sound is necessary to lure or distract the enemy. As always, save the mission often.

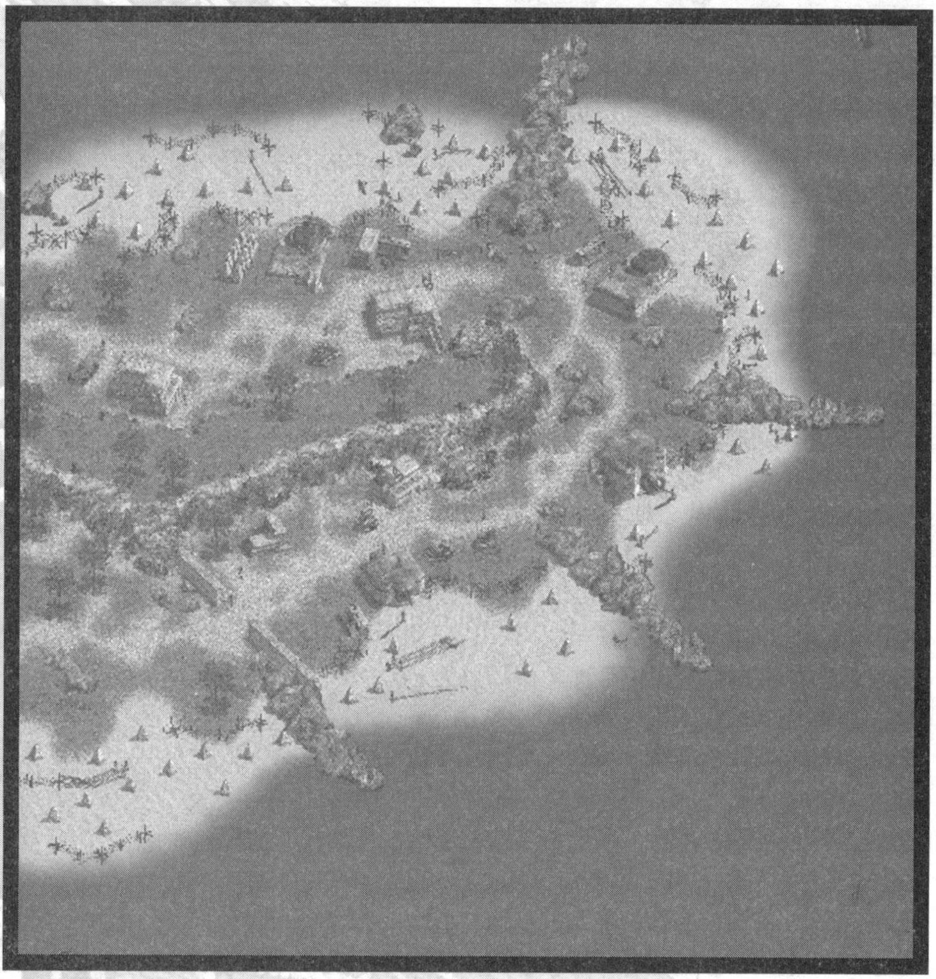

Figure 6-8. D-Day Kick-Off

PHASE 1: THE LANDING

Your team of Commandos begins in a light boat in the southwest corner of the map. You must get them all to dry land, but enemy soldiers patrol the landing area. Have the Marine don his diving gear and go over the side of the boat. Swim to where Patrol 1 makes its turn to the west, around the concrete dragon's tooth. As they pass you, pop out of the water and shoot one of the rear soldiers with the speargun.

Figure 6-9.
The Marine must clear the beach so the other Commandos can land safely.

Quickly submerge. When they turn again, take out the second soldier with the speargun and the third with the pistol; then return to the water and swim back to the boat. Patrol 3 will spot the bodies and go to investigate; however, they simply return to their patrol without sounding the alarm.

TIP

The Marine should practice swimming next to an enemy positioned near the water, popping up and killing the soldier with the speargun, and then immediately returning to the water. This method is especially useful for killing groups of soldiers such as patrols.

Now the Marine can row the boat to shore. Tie it up as far west as possible and get the team out. While everyone else lies prone, send the Green Beret and Sapper crawling to hide behind the rock to the north when the patrol isn't looking. Then have the Green Beret approach the ridge and climb up the side as the patrol heads away. Knife Soldier 2 at the top and then go prone. The Sapper now can position the trap along the patrol's route north of his hiding place. After it kills one soldier, reset it in the same place to kill a second. The Green Beret can kill the third if he begins descending the ridge as the patrol of two approaches the trap. Finally, get all the rest of the Commandos behind the rock as the Sapper recovers his trap.

PHASE 2: THE FIRST GUN EMPLACEMENT

Now your team is ready to clear the area around the first gun emplacement. The Green Beret begins by placing the decoy in the northern corner of the wall and moving away from it. While prone, activate the decoy and lure Soldier 4 into the open. Sneak up behind him and use the knife. Recover the decoy, place it at the south end of the wall near Soldier 7, and then return to the northern wall. Now the Sniper must crawl out from behind the rock and set his sights on Soldier 5, walking along the top of the gun emplacement. When no one is watching 5, shoot him, drop prone, and crawl back behind the rock.

Figure 6-10. Your team must clear all enemy soldiers from the area before the Sapper can place an explosive near the gun emplacement.

The Green Beret now climbs over the wall and hides behind the small blockhouse. Activate the decoy to lure Soldier 7 around the wall; then run after and knife 6, pick up the body, walk toward 7, drop the body past the wall and knife 7. Watch out for Patrol 12 and Soldier 14 as you do this. The Green Beret must move quickly to get to Soldier 7 before he loses interest in the decoy.

The entrance is clear, so the Green Beret can crawl to the gun emplacement and scale up the side while Patrol 12 and soldiers 13 and 14 aren't looking. Stay prone at the top and then knife 8 and 9. Make sure no soldiers are watching your targets as you kill them or they'll sound the alarm.

Climb down from the emplacement and crawl over to the block house to the northwest. When 10 and 11 walk away from you, run after and knife 10; then carry the body behind the barracks. Place the decoy west of the barracks hiding place and lure Soldier 11 to where you can kill him. Hide the body.

The Green Beret now must move back out though the wall and place the decoy near the southern part of the wall. Move the bodies of 6 and 7 out of sight. The Sapper must place the trap in the path to the decoy and then return to hiding. With the Marine in the water nearby, activate the decoy and hide the Green Beret in the sand. When Patrol 12 comes to see what's happening, one of them walks into the trap. The Marine and Green Beret can kill the rest. Use pistols on the last one to lure soldiers 13 and 14. Hide the Green Beret and Marine again and repeat the process with these two curious Germans.

The Green Beret must crawl back into the base and place the decoy behind the rock near Soldier 17 before crawling back to a position behind 15. Activate the decoy to distract 16 and 17 so you can knife 15. Then run and kill 16 and 17. Move all the bodies out of sight. Have the Marine swim near 18, pop out of the water, and kill the machine-gunner with the speargun when he's not looking.

Bring the rest of the Commando team up to the first gun emplacement. Be sure the Sapper retrieves his trap. Then place the first explosive next to the gun at the emplacement—but don't detonate it yet. Save it for the grand finale. One down, three to go.

TIP

Usually, you want to avoid using the pistol during a mission. Because you must fire three times to kill an enemy, it can be dangerous, and the report often alerts other enemies to your presence. They may sound an alarm. Sometimes, however, you can use gunshots to lure soldiers into traps and ambushes. A good rule of thumb is to save the mission, and then fire a pistol to test the enemy's response.

PHASE 3: THE EASTERN SECTOR

Now the Sapper and Green Beret must set up a deadly surprise for Soldier 19. While the Sapper places the trap between the rocks and the barbed wire, the Green Beret positions the decoy west of 19. The Sapper returns to hide near the gun emplacement while the Green Beret activates the decoy and quickly hides himself in the sand. After 19 dies, retrieve the trap and decoy.

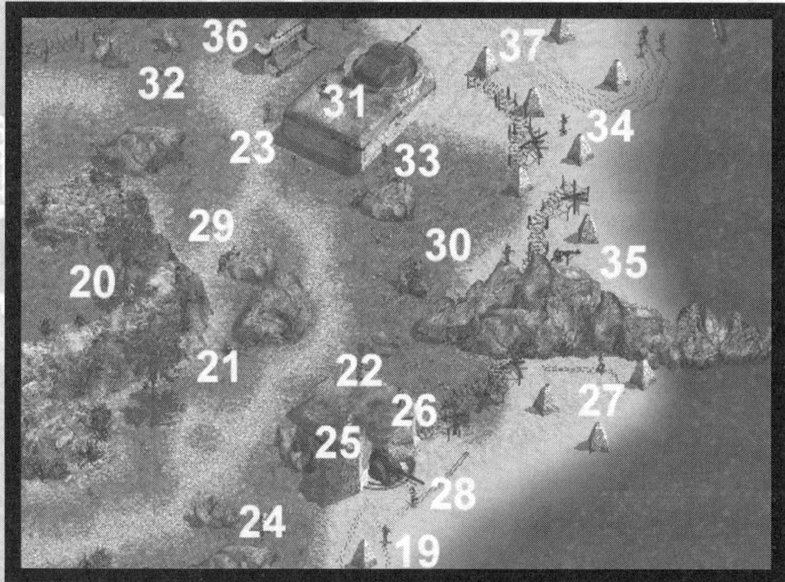

Figure 6-11. More than 20 soldiers protect the two gun emplacements in this area. Work carefully!

Now send the Green Beret up the ridge near the barracks. Crawl over to Soldier 20 and knife him when 22 isn't looking. Wait until 22, 23, and 27 look away before descending the cliff near 21 to hide behind the rock. Knife 21 when 22 and 24 won't see, and then carry the body behind the rock. Bring out the Sniper and move him around to the north side of the first gun emplacement. Have him shoot 22 when 24 isn't looking. Drop prone and bring up the precision rifle again. Soldier 23 will spot 24's body and go over to investigate. Shoot him when he's right over the body.

NOTE

The rear of the second gun emplacement is level with the ground, enabling a Commando to walk to the top without climbing walls. This also means enemy soldiers at ground level behind the emplacement have a good view of the entire roof.

The Green Beret now must crawl west and sneak up on 24. Kill him while 27 and 28 are turned away. Now crawl up onto the second gun emplacement and kill 25 and 26. Have the Marine swim over near Soldier 27 while the Green Beret hides on the west side of the second gun emplacement. As he begins walking away, pop out of the water, run after him, and take him out with the speargun. Drop prone.

Soldier 28 will see the body and walk over to it. This is the Green Beret's chance to run after and kill 28 with the knife. Next, crawl behind the rock near the machine-gunner (29). Kill him and remove the body without 33 spotting you. Again, bring all your Commandos forward and hide them near the second gun emplacement. The Sapper should take this opportunity to set the second explosive the same way he did the first.

Now the Green Beret must place the decoy south of Soldier 30 while the Sapper places the trap in the gap to the west. Lure 30 into the trap, then recover trap, body, and decoy so all are out of sight. Position the Sniper east of the gun emplacement, behind the barbed wire, and shoot Soldier 31 when 32 and 34 look away. Drop prone while Green Beret and Sapper place the trap and a body south of the rock by 30 so that 32 can see it, but not 33 and 34. Soldier 32 will walk into the trap and be killed.

Now the Sniper must take out 33 at the west end of his patrol. The Marine must swim over near Soldier 34. After Patrol 37 passes heading north, rise from the water and kill 34 with the speargun, and then 35, as well. While the Marine re-enters the water, the Green Beret must move quickly to carry 34's body, and then 35's, behind the dragon's tooth near 35 so Patrol 37 won't see them and raise an alarm.

Have the Green Beret crawl over behind the wall near 36. Wait until Patrol 37 passes by heading south, and then kill 36 at the east end of his walk. Carry the body to the ladder at the third gun emplacement. Finally, order the Marine to swim around the north shore and wait just off the beach in the northwest.

PHASE 4: THE NORTHERN SECTOR

This is another phase that requires teamwork and timing. The Green Beret starts by placing the decoy east of Soldier 38. Lure him around the corner and kill him with the knife. Carry the body over near the third gun emplacement. Now sneak up on 39, knife him when no one is looking, and carry the body to the gap between the barracks and the rocks. This also will be your main hiding place in this phase. Have

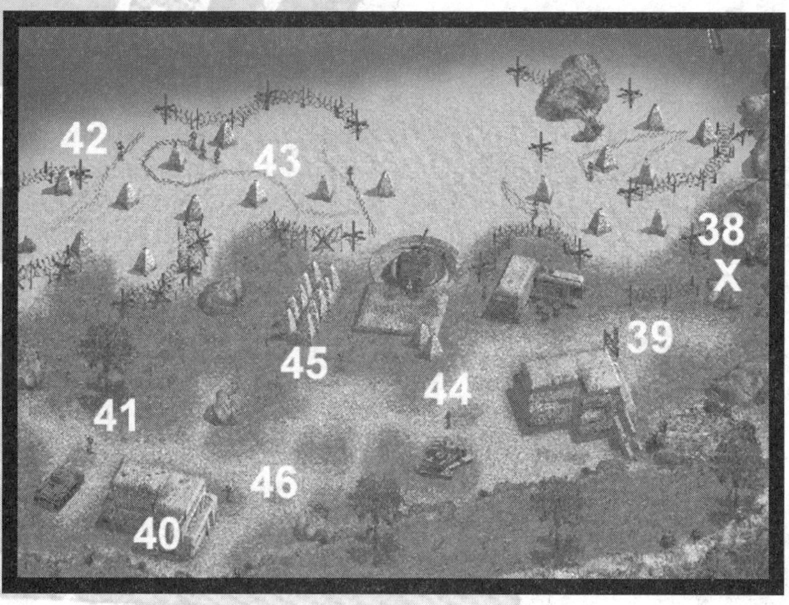

Figure 6-12. This northern sector is full of enemy troops. You needn't kill them all covertly, however. After you get the Driver to the tank in the west, you can make all the noise you want.

the Sapper climb up the third gun emplacement and set his last explosive next to the gun. Then send the Sapper, the Driver, and the Sniper to hide with the Green Beret.

For the next few steps, the Marine will work alone. Wait until Patrol 43 heads east and 42 passes by moving southwest. Jump out of the water at the far west end of the beach and make tracks in the sand. Hop back into the water and swim east a bit so you have a straight shot to the grass. Soldier 42 will see your footprints and go take a look. As he moves past your position, crawl out of the water toward the rock by 41 as quickly as you can. You want to end up along the western map edge.

When 40 isn't looking, sneak behind the building near the tank into the little alcove where you can hide from 40. Stand up, wait for Soldier 40 to approach, and then turn around. Quickly run after and knife him. Next, kill Soldier 41, and then crawl over near the rock. Soldier 42 will see the body and go to investigate. Shoot him with the speargun as he walks past the rock. Now the Marine must crawl back behind the building and along the ridge to position himself behind the crates near 44.

This next step is very difficult, so save the mission here. The Sniper now must crawl to position 'X' in figure 6-12. He must be able to target 44 unseen by the soldiers patrolling the beach. When Patrol 43 has passed the fourth gun emplacement heading west, 45 is moving west, and 46 isn't looking, the Marine must shoot 44 with the speargun, and then crawl back behind the crates. Quickly switch to the Sniper and target the area around 44. Shoot 45 and 46 before they can sound the alarm, dropping prone after each shot. Then crawl back to the hiding place as fast as you can. Patrol 43 will spot the bodies in a few seconds and sound the alarm. The Sapper can now detonate all three explosives and then drop back down to the ground.

Reinforcements now pour out of the barracks. If all your Commandos remain hidden, no one will spot them. After the new patrols pass your location, the Driver must crawl around the barracks and along the ridge to the tank.

PHASE 5: ARMORED MAYHEM

When the Driver is aboard the tank, get it going. Move east, taking out all enemies in the area. Take care not to blow up the explosive barrels during the firefight. Soldiers will pour out of the barracks like crazy. Kill them all.

Figure 6-13.
The Driver, at the tank's controls, clears the rest of the map for you.

When the area is clear, get all the Commandos onto the tank, except the Green Beret. He must move one of the barrels over to the fourth gun emplacement and detonate it with a pistol shot. Then get him aboard the tank. Drive the tank back to where you left the boat, taking out all German soldiers along the way. Once the entire map is clear, get your Commandos to the boat and the Marine will row it to the safety of the buoy in the southeast.

MISSION 15: THE END OF THE BUTCHER

FRANCE, AUGUST 26, 1944

Paris welcomes a triumphant General de Gaulle, leader of the Free France movement. German troops have retreated northeast. One of the first high commands to leave Paris was the SS *Grupenfuhrer* Helmut Schleper, called the "Butcher of Paris" for his outrages against members of the French Resistance.

Fleeing judgment, Schleper has withdrawn to the village of Compiegne. He departs for Berlin tomorrow morning with a list of names of members of the German Resistance. You must liquidate him before he and his list can reach Berlin.

MISSION SUMMARY

Objective: Kill the SS *Grupenfuhrer* and destroy the headquarters building.

Team: Sniper, Marine, Driver, Spy

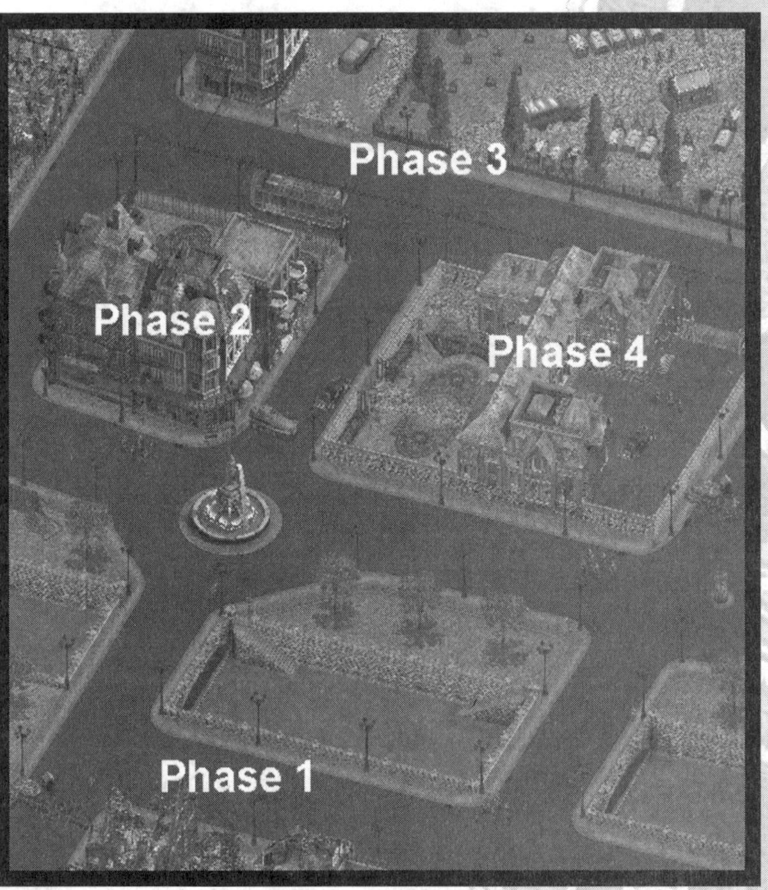

Figure 6-14. The city is full of soldiers. You must remain unnoticed because the guards sound the alarm with little provocation.

This mission is basically an assassination. Command also orders you to blow up the headquarters building while you're in the area. Your Commandos begin along the southern map edge. They first must get across the river and acquire a German uniform for the Spy. Then they must get to the northern part of the map unseen and find a way to blow up the headquarters and kill the SS officer. Finally, they must escape in the truck.

PHASE 1: CROSSING THE RIVER

Your Commandos begin in the center of the southern map edge, behind some junked automobiles. German soldiers are posted all around you. Your Spy must do a lot of the killing during this mission; however, he lacks a uniform. That makes this first phase difficult, but not impossible. The Spy starts by making his way into the building west of the automobiles. Watch out for soldiers 1 and 2 and Patrol 7. When they all move away from this area, enter the building and hide in the northwest corner. Wait until Soldier 1 walks into the building, and then use the syringe of poison on him. Carry the body into the corner. Soldier 2 is your next target, but you pause first until Patrol 7 completes its round and passes heading west. Sneak up behind 2, poison him, and carry the body to the corner in the building where you dumped 1.

Figure 6-15. The streets are full of guards—and there are few places to hide.

TIP

There are many soldiers in the southern area, and a lot of open space. Before you take any actions, save the mission, and then take time to observe what each enemy can see and the routes they walk. When you have a good feel for their actions and the timing necessary to get by them, restart the mission from your save. This way, you avoid wasting time looking around, and will receive more points for completing the mission faster.

After Patrol 7 passes again, the Spy must head east. He can move in behind Soldier 3 and poison him when soldiers 8 and 9 and Patrol 10 look the other way. Carry the body to the southeast corner and hide it there. Stay prone with the body until Patrol 7 makes another round. Then head back to the other Commandos.

Figure 6-16. Several soldiers patrol the southeastern section of the map, but you must kill only one.

While the Spy is returning, send the Marine crawling across the eastern bridge and down the stairs to the river, unnoticed by soldiers in the area. Don the diving gear and swim to the western stairs. Wait until Soldier 4 comes down and then begins going back up before you pop out of the water and shoot him with the spear-gun. You must kill 4 as close to the water as you can so his body won't be visible to other soldiers.

Now the Spy can crawl west and hide by the river's south shore, along the western map edge. Wait for Soldier 5 to move south past you; then sneak up behind him and kill him while he pauses at the end of his route. Quickly carry the body into the building and hide it in the corner with the other two bodies before Patrol 7 spots you. After the patrol passes, crawl to a position near Soldier 6. Wait until no one is looking, and then kill 7 and carry the body down the steps to where the Marine killed Soldier 4. Keep the Spy on the ground.

PHASE 2: GETTING THE UNIFORM

The Spy must cross a well-guarded street to get to the German uniform. When the coast is clear, crawl up the stairs and west to hide near the fence. When Soldier 13 begins walking west, and other soldiers aren't looking, run as fast as you can to the ladder below the uniform. Climb it. By the time 13 turns around, the Spy will be an SS general. Descend the ladder and kill 13, careful to carry his body behind the fence before Patrol 17 sees it. Then climb back up the ladder and kill 14 at the western

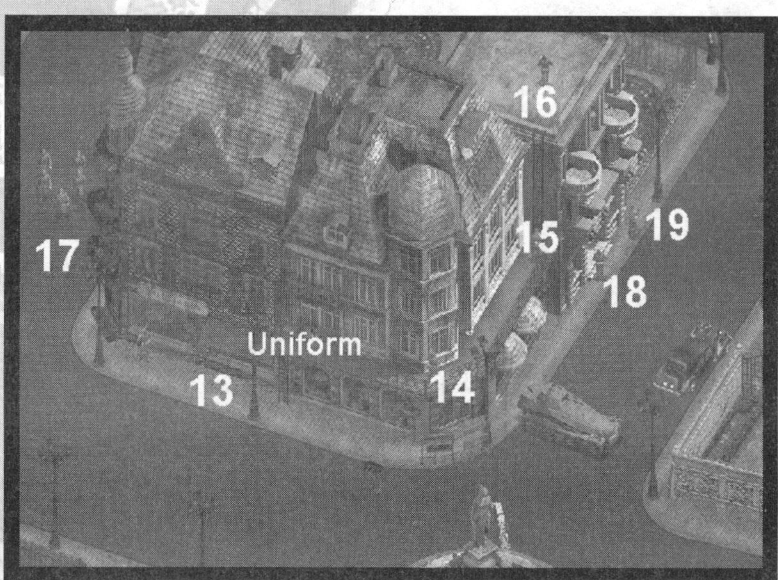

Figure 6-17. You'll find the Uniform on the second-floor landing. Once you have it on, use it to clear off the soldiers on the buildings in this block.

end of his route, and then 15. Leave the bodies where they lie. As long as no one saw you kill them, they won't be visible from street level. Next, climb the ladder to the next building and give 16 a lethal injection. You must time this carefully, so the soldier in the headquarters yard doesn't see.

Climb back down to the street and use the Spy to distract Patrol 7 so the rest of the Commandos can crawl over and hide behind the fence on the north side of the river in the west. When soldiers 9 and 12 walk away, get the Commandos into the building near the half-track, below where you killed 14.

You got the whole team across the river. Take a deep breath and get ready for the next phase.

PHASE 3: SETTING UP FOR THE KILL

With the Sniper, Marine, and Driver all safe in the corner building, the Spy can break off his conversation with Patrol 7 and walk over to the fountain. Wait for Patrol 17 to arrive, and then keep them facing anywhere between east and south.

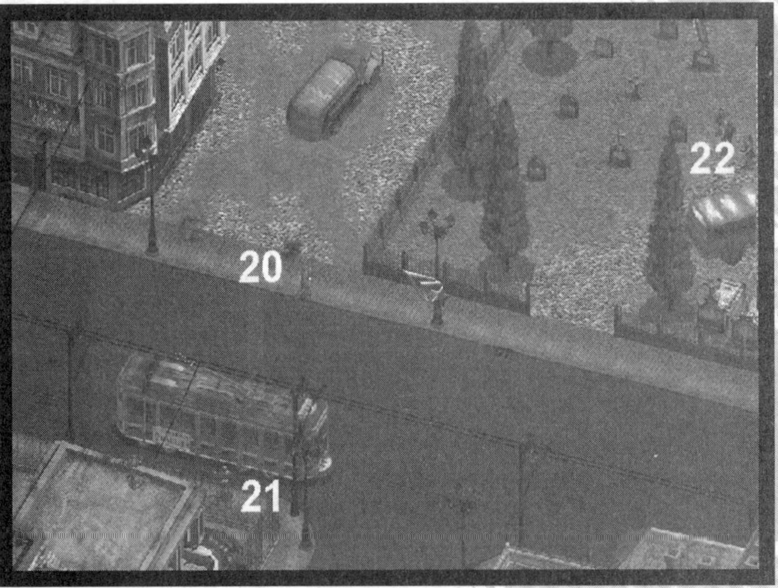

Figure 6-18. There aren't as many soldiers in the north. However, there are few places for your Commandos to hide, and almost none for concealing enemy bodies.

When soldiers 9, 12, and Patrol 7 are walking away, the three hidden Commandos can exit the building and crawl west, and then north. Keep an eye on Soldier 20. When he begins walking east, you can crawl and hide behind the west side of the building, near the red fuel truck. Now watch Soldier 21. Rush into the building as 20 walks away and 21 looks away.

Then the Spy can leave Patrol 17 and walk north past the headquarters and then east, to the rear of the building. Walk to Soldier 23 and kill him while Patrol 25 heads south. Time is short, so you must move fast, carry the body out the gate, and drop it west of the gate. Next, walk into the cemetery and stand behind Soldier 24. Poison him as Patrol 22 heads west and carry the body a bit north to hide it behind the sepulchres, near the eastern map edge. When you're done, walk over and talk to Soldier 21. Keep his attention to the east.

Work quickly during this next step, or the entire mission could end in failure. Wait for Patrol 17 to come north. When it turns and heads back south, the Marine must move out of the building when Soldier 20 turns east. Run after 20 and kill him with the speargun. Then kill 21 as the Spy talks to him. The soldier that passes the headquarters gates can see the body, so you must time it just right, allowing the Spy enough time to move the body west and out of sight. Then, while the Marine returns to the building, the Spy must run south to meet Patrol 17 near the fountain and continue his conversation where he left off.

Figure 6-19. The Spy and the Sniper must clear the area behind the headquarters.

Take another deep breath. It's the Sniper's turn. Exit the building and have the Sniper crawl all the way to the eastern map edge, along the sidewalk on the north side of the road. Patrol 22 is the only threat to watch for. Position the Sniper so he has a good view of the headquarters parking area. When Patrol 25 heads south in a straight line, bring up the precision rifle and kill all three soldiers in sequence, beginning with the one at the rear. You must shoot quickly to kill them all before they can

TIP

When the Sniper takes out Patrol 25, he needn't go prone between each shot. No one can see him where he is, and he must shoot all three soldiers very quickly.

Figure 6-20. You must park the fuel truck just inside the gate, next to the headquarters. When it blows up, it will block the SS officers' primary evacuation route.

sound the alarm. And make every shot count. The Sniper has only four bullets, and he needs the last bullet to assassinate the SS officer. After eliminating the patrol, crawl back to the building.

Now the Driver can leave his hiding place and crawl to the fuel truck. Wait until Patrol 22 turns away, and then hop in. Back it out onto the road; then drive it east to the parking lot. Try to drive alongside the trolley as it heads east to conceal the truck from soldiers near the half-track. Park just inside the gate, next to the headquarters, as shown in figure 6-20. Leave the truck and crawl over to the German army truck in the cemetery.

PHASE 4: THE KILL

The Driver must wait for Patrol 22 to head east before jumping into the truck. Quickly, but carefully, back it out through the cemetery gate; then drive it over to the building where the Marine and Sniper wait. Keep the engine running: once the fun starts, you must make a quick getaway.

Move the Sniper back outside and position him in the area where the fuel truck was parked originally, so he has a good view of the headquarters main gate. He must be able to shoot the SS officer as he walks through the gate toward the black car parked at the curb.

The Spy can now end his conversation with Patrol 17. Send him running toward the waiting truck. Then exit the Marine from the building. Before he hops in the truck, have him fire a pistol shot into the air to trigger an alarm. The fuel truck will explode when reinforcements pour out the back door of the headquarters.

Cut off from his primary escape route, the SS officer will head for the car out front. The Sniper must shoot him before he can get into the car. Then quickly get the Sniper into the truck with the rest of your team. As soon as the Sniper is aboard, the Driver can hit the gas and steer the truck around the corner, heading north and off the map to safety.

MISSION 16: STOP WILDFIRE

BELGIUM, SEPTEMBER 4, 1944

The Allies begin a rapid advance across Belgium. A strong determination leads the Allied command to cross the Rhine. Preparations for Operation Market Garden are underway.

As German forces retreat behind the Siegfried Line, they'll try to demolish the bridge over the Maas River, north of Liege, to thwart Allied troops. Your mission is to prevent them from doing so.

MISSION SUMMARY

Objective: Kill all the German sappers before they can blow the bridge over the Maas.

Team: Sniper, Marine, Spy

This mission may not be as difficult as some, it does require very precise timing. Your Commandos begin in the northeast. They must make their way to the bridge undetected, kill all four sappers before they can blow the bridge, and escape in the army truck. The trick is that you must kill the sappers with a few seconds of each other. If even one detonates his explosive, the mission fails. You also must use stealth. It won't take much to provoke the soldiers into sounding the alarm—and send the

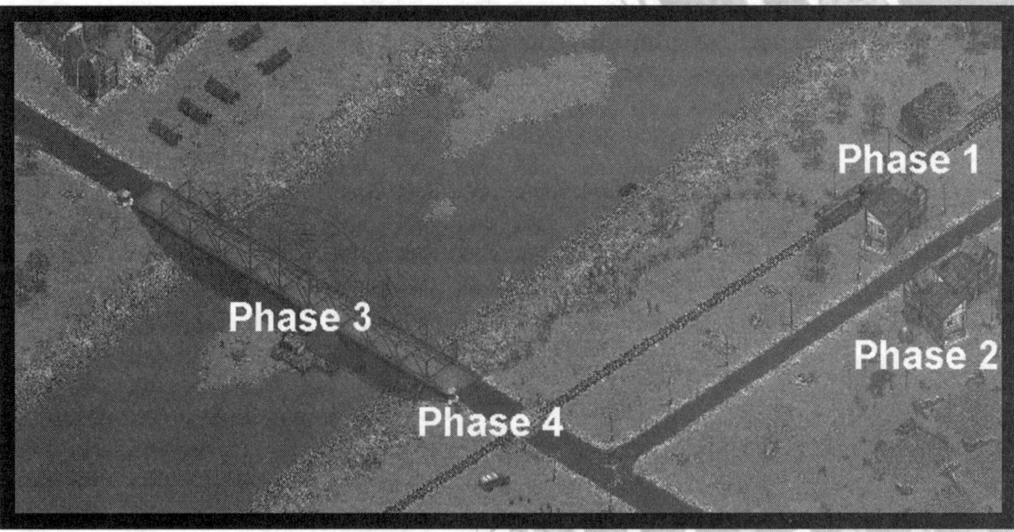

Figure 6-21. Your Commandos must kill all four sappers near the bridge simultaneously.

sappers to their detonators. Notice that the map is full of enemy soldiers. However, you needn't kill them all to complete the mission.

PHASE 1: THE TRAIN STATION

Your three Commandos begin in the northeast corner of the map. The first step is to clear the train station of soldiers. While the Sniper and Marine stay prone, the Spy approaches the station from the west. Hide behind the western corner, until the train stops at the station. Then poison Soldier 1 as he walks toward the train. Carry his body behind the station before soldiers 3 and 4 can discover it when the train leaves. When the next train stops, kill Soldier 2. You must approach from the southwest, because there's no access to him from the north. Move the body out of sight, as previously. Now crawl to Soldier 3, careful to stay out view of Soldier 4. When 4 walks away from you, kill 3 and hide the body north of the tracks. Kill Soldier 4 on

> **CAUTION**
> Your men must take care crossing the railroad tracks, especially near the eastern map edge. A train can appear at any moment, without warning. If it strikes a Commando, he dies.

Figure 6-22. Use the train for cover while it's stopped at the station.

Figure 6-23. Now you must kill all the guards around the building near the road, south of the train station.

his next trip southwest and leave his body where it lies.

Now the Spy can make his way south to hide north of the building near the road. Wait until both soldiers 5 and 7 head southwest, and then poison 5 and carry his body around the corner of the building. Go around to the other side and kill Soldier 6 when 7 again heads away from you. Move his body over near 5's, and then hide inside the building. Again, Soldier 7 will walk up to the building. As he turns around, run out the door, poison him, and dispose of the body.

PHASE 2: ACQUIRE A GERMAN UNIFORM

The Spy forgot his German uniform again, so you must steal one from a clothesline. Move over near the buildings to the east. Hide out of view of Soldier 8. When he and Soldier 10 both walk away from you, kill 8 and carry his body north and out of sight.

Next, crawl around to the southern corner of the building, near 8's post. Wait until Soldier 10 and Patrol 11 both move away from the clothesline. Then run and grab the uniform quickly. You have just enough time to put it on before the patrol

Figure 6-24.
The uniform hangs on a clothesline near the courtyard.

turns the corner and spots you. Now walk over to Soldier 9, near the barracks. Approach him from behind and poison him. Leave the body and wait for Soldier 12, (figure 6-25) to spot it and come to investigate. Poison him when he looks away. Leave both bodies and walk toward the wall along 10's route. You must kill him so the body drops in the corner of the wall, out of sight of Patrol 11.

PHASE 3: THE SAPPER MUST DIE

It's time for your Commando team to move out. Send the uniformed Spy across the bridge. No one will stop him or even look twice. The Marine must make his way to the river, don the diving gear, and then swim down to the river. Finally, the Sniper can follow the road the Spy cleared to the south. Past the building near Patrol 11, drop prone and crawl past the bunker where Soldier 9 died, and then directly south. At the map edge, carefully crawl west so you can sight the barrels near the truck with the precision rifle. This should be just east of the road. Wait until Patrol 13 makes its rounds and is near the barrels, heading west. Shoot all four soldiers so their bodies lie south of the barrels. Fire quickly and carefully before they can cry for help. The Sniper has only five bullets this mission. You mustn't waste any on the patrol, because the fifth bullet is for a sapper. The Sniper is positioned far enough from other soldiers in the area that he needn't crouch between shots. Speed, not stealth, is crucial here.

Figure 6-25. The Sniper will work the east side of the bridge.

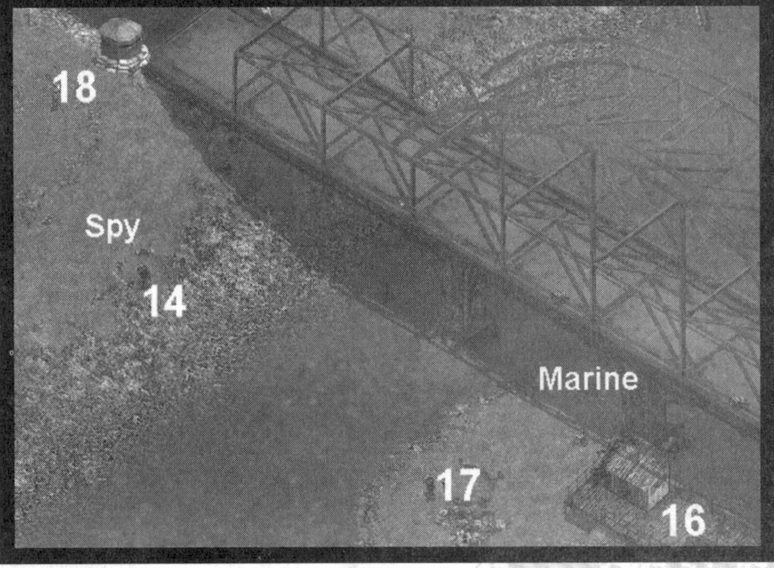

Figure 6-26. Positioning your Commandos is critical. Once the alarm goes off, they must kill the sappers from these positions: they have no time to move.

After eliminating the patrol, crawl forward to target the space directly in front of the pillbox near the bridge. Keeping the rifle sighted on this area, go to the Marine. Position this Commando in the little inlet near the detonator on the island under the bridge. Put him in a shallow area so the diving gear shows in his knapsack. Finally, move the Spy directly behind Sapper 14. It's a good idea to save the mission here: the next step requires perfect timing.

With all three Commandos in position, it's time to kill the sappers. When Soldier 18 and the patrol on the west side of the river, as well as Sapper 17 on the island, look away, the Spy must poison Sapper 14 quickly. One down. Put the syringe away and switch to the Sniper ([2]). Drop Sapper 15 as he walks past the pillbox; then drop prone. Quickly shift to the Marine ([3]). Pop out of the water and shoot sappers 16 and 17 with the pistol before they can reach the detonator. Remember, it takes three shots to kill each of them. With all four sappers dead, get back into the water and swim to the southern map edge near the east shore of the river.

TIP

Before killing the sappers, you may want to test their response to an alarm. Save the mission, have a Commando fire a pistol, and watch the fireworks start. Pay close attention to the order in which the sappers detonate their explosives. This illustrates the importance of acting quickly, as well as the order in which you must kill them.

PHASE 4: THE GETAWAY

As the Marine swims for shore, the Spy can cross back over the bridge. Keep the Marine and Sniper hidden as the Spy walks over to Soldier 19. When Soldier 20 and Patrol 25 walk away, poison 19 and leave the body. Soldier 20 will see it and go to take a look. When the patrol heads away again, approach 20 from behind and kill him, as well.

Now walk back onto the edge of the bridge. Kill 21 when soldiers 22 and 24 and Patrol 26 aren't looking. Next, kill 22, then 23, and, finally, 24 — each while it's safe to do so. Don't worry about an alarm; it's already gone off. As long as no one sees the Spy kill the soldiers, the enemy won't go after him.

Figure 6-27. The Spy must kill several soldiers near the eastern edge of the bridge to make the escape less dangerous.

With only the two patrols remaining near the bridge, the Spy now should walk over and distract Patrol 25's attention north and away from the truck. This will allow the Sniper and the Marine to crawl over next to it. The Spy then can break off the conversation and walk to the truck, as well. When patrols 25 and 26 both walk away from the truck, get all three Commandos aboard. The truck will take them to safety.

MISSION 17: BEFORE DAWN

FRANCE, NOVEMBER 28, 1944

Despite the failure of Operation Market Garden, the Allied forces continue their drive toward the Rhine. At this point, France is not yet entirely liberated. In Riveauville, a small town north of Colmar, the French Resistance leader Claude Gilbert has been arrested along with some of his followers. He'll be executed tomorrow at dawn.

Your mission is to free the prisoners and bring them to Allied lines safe and sound.

MISSION SUMMARY

Objective: Free Claude Gilbert and his four collaborators and get them all to safety.

Team: Green Beret, Marine, Spy

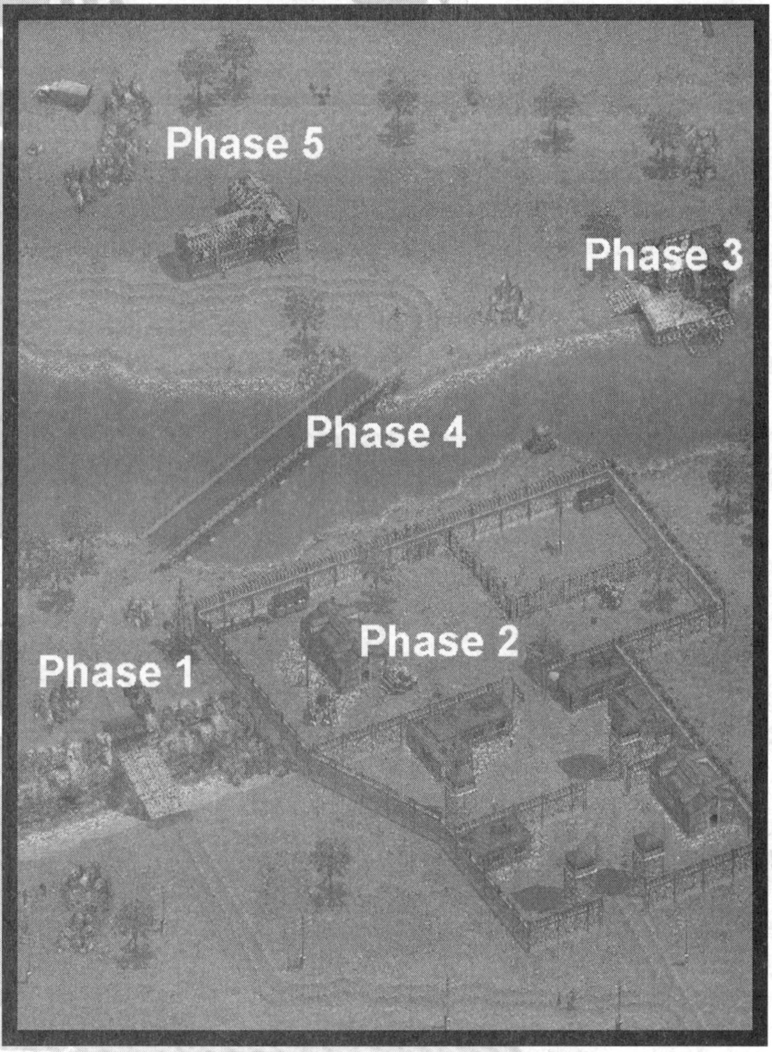

Figure 6-28.
Before Dawn

This mission isn't difficult as long as you play carefully. Your Commandos begin in the southwest. You must clear the area west of the prison before securing the prison interior and releasing the Frenchmen. You also must clear the north side of the river so you can bring your charges unharmed to the truck that will carry you all to safety. The prisoners can't crawl, so you'll have to kill most of the Germans on the map.

PHASE 1: THE MOBILE BRIDGE

Your Commandos begin in the southwestern part of the map. Luckily, the Spy brought a German uniform this time. Put him to work right away, sending him east along the road. With the disguise, he'll have little trouble walking right into the prison. Don't bother killing anybody yet. Instead, walk straight to the back gate near the river. To open it, click the control box on the wall left of the gate. Head west to the mobile bridge and click on the controls in the nearby truck to slide it across.

Walk over to Soldier 2 and keep him occupied while the Green Beret crawls across the bridge (after the patrol heads back toward the prison) and knifes Soldier 1.

Figure 6-29. Four soldiers guard the area around the mobile bridge.

Watch for Soldier 3 during this. Then carry the body behind the rock near Soldier 2. Next, kill 2 while the Spy distracts him, and remove the body. Now the Spy must distract Soldier 4 so the Green Beret can kill 3. Again, hide the body behind the rock. Finally, have the Spy poison Soldier 4 unseen by patrols 16 and 17. Dispose of the body and send the Marine across the bridge, as well. Hide the Green Beret and Marine near the bodies as the Spy slides the bridge back so no one else can cross it.

PHASE 2: THE PRISON YARD

The Spy had better make sure his syringe is full of poison: he'll need it for this phase. Send him back into the prison yard and close the gate behind him. No one will get in or out until he's finished. Soldier 5 patrols back and forth between 6 and 7. Kill him when he's halfway between them on his way toward 6. Carry the body and hide it behind the shower near 6. Move behind 6 and kill him as Soldier 9 walks away. Again, hide the body behind the shower. Walk over to Soldier 7 and pause for a moment. Check out what Soldier 8 can see by Shift-clicking on him. When he turns and walks away, kill 8 and move the body south, to just inside 8's view. Soldier 8 will notice the body and walk over to investigate. Poison him as he looks at the body. Soldier 9 may be able to see these bodies. If not, move them so he can. Then kill 9 when *he* comes over to take a look. See? This is pretty easy.

Figure 6-30.
The prison yard is full of soldiers. The Spy must kill them all—all by himself.

Time to clear out the other side of the yard. Walk over to Soldier 10. When 11 isn't looking, pull out the poison and give 10 a lethal injection. Soldier 11 will see the body and walk to it, giving you a perfect opportunity to kill him. Now walk over to Soldier 12, near the cell. When 13 is turned away, kill 12. Then maneuver behind 13 and kill him. All the guards are dead, but you have a few more things to do before you release the prisoners.

Near the entrance into the rest of the camp is a fuel tank. The Spy must climb the ladder and open the valve. When you place the cursor over the tank, it changes to the hand-and-lever. Click several times, until the fuel pours onto the ground in a steady stream. We'll come back to this later.

PHASE 3: THE OLD MILL

Now walk to the back gate and open it again. Head across the bridge to the eastern map edge. Wait for Soldier 14 to walk behind the building, and then kill him. Dump the body in the river. Soldier 15 should be able to see the body. If not, move

Figure 6-31. The Spy must kill these two soldiers so the prisoners can leave their cell unobserved.

it a bit so he goes to check it out. Kill him and put both bodies into the river. This helps ensure the next step will go unobserved. Walk back across the bridge and over to Patrol 16.

The Spy must keep Patrol 16 east of the gate and looking east. This gives the Green Beret a chance to crawl into the prison camp while Patrol 17 heads north across the bridge. When the Green Beret is inside and out of sight, the Spy can break off his conversation and let the patrol head west. Distract them again west of the gate so they're looking away from it. Now the Green Beret can release the prisoners.

March them carefully out the gate and along the wall to the east. Make sure no one across the river is watching—namely, Patrol 17 and Soldier 18. Hide the prisoners along the east wall of the prison. The Green Beret now must use his strength to pick up the explosive barrel near the cell gate and position it directly behind the bunker. He must be very careful of Soldier 18. If he shoots at the Green Beret, the barrel probably will be hit and your man will be toast—literally. After the barrel is in place, move the Green Beret over near the prisoners.

CAUTION

You must be very careful moving the prisoners. They can't crawl (but they can run), and anyone looking in their direction will see them. Give orders to Claude. When he moves, the other four will follow in a line. They look a lot like a caterpillar moving across the map.

PHASE 4: EXPLOSIONS AND GUNSHOTS

When the Green Beret and the Frenchmen are out of sight, the Spy can leave Patrol 16 and walk into the base. While no one is looking, pull the pistol from his holster and fire at the puddle of fuel pouring out of the tanks. The bullet will ignite it and the tank will provide the fuel to keep it burning. If that doesn't bring Patrol 16 into the yard, fire a couple of shots near the gate. Position the Spy along the wall so he can shoot each soldier in the patrol as he walks through the gate. (Remember, you must shoot each soldier three times to kill him.)

Figure 6-32. You must clear both sides of the river before you can take the prisoners across the bridge.

Now the Green Beret can crawl around the corner of the prison wall and fire at the explosive barrel. Drop prone and crawl back into hiding. The barrel will destroy the bunker and alert those on the other side of the river to your presence. Not only will Patrol 17 come to investigate, but so will soldiers 18, 19, 20, and 21. Run to the bridge and poison the soldiers at the end of the line, one at a time. You should

TIP

The Marine really isn't necessary for this mission, but you can use him to fire the pistol from hiding and keep the soldiers and the patrol from crossing back over the bridge. He can even help gun down the patrol.

be able to get two as they move east and two more after they turn back around and head west. All that should be left is the patrol. Hide the Spy behind the rock near the bridge and lure the patrol to you with pistol shots. Position the Spy so he's around a corner and can fire at the patrol one soldier at a time. When the patrol is dead, you can begin the mission's final phase.

PHASE 5: OVER THE RIVER AND TO THE TRUCK

Now the Spy must do some mopping up across the river. Walk across the bridge and over to Soldier 22. Kill him, and then kill Machine-gunner 23 when Patrol 26 heads away from you. Move the body over near 22's.

It's time to get the Marine, Green Beret, and prisoners to the south side of the bridge.

With the riverfront clear, you need only secure the path to the truck. Move the Spy over near Soldier 24. When Patrol 26 heads east and 25 looks away, poison 24, and then kill 25. Move both bodies into the corner of the building. Then run after Patrol 26. Distract their attention toward the northeast, away from the bridge and truck.

Time to get the Green Beret, the Marine, and the Frenchmen across the river and into the truck. When all are safely aboard, get the Spy into the truck and it will take them all to safety.

Figure 6-33. Kill these two soldiers and distract the patrol to clear the path to the truck.

MISSION 18: THE FORCE OF CIRCUMSTANCE

FRANCE, DECEMBER 16, 1944

Today Hitler deploys a surprise operation. German reserves break through Allied defenses in the Ardennes region and soon takes Liege. The Battle of the Bulge has begun.

To cut off the rapid advance of enemy reinforcements, a small Commando team will infiltrate north of Liege and blow up the bridge over the Maas River. Coincidentally, the men best-prepared to do the job are the ones who defended it back in September—you.

MISSION SUMMARY

Objective: Destroy the bridge over the River Maas.

Team: Green Beret, Marine, Sapper, Driver

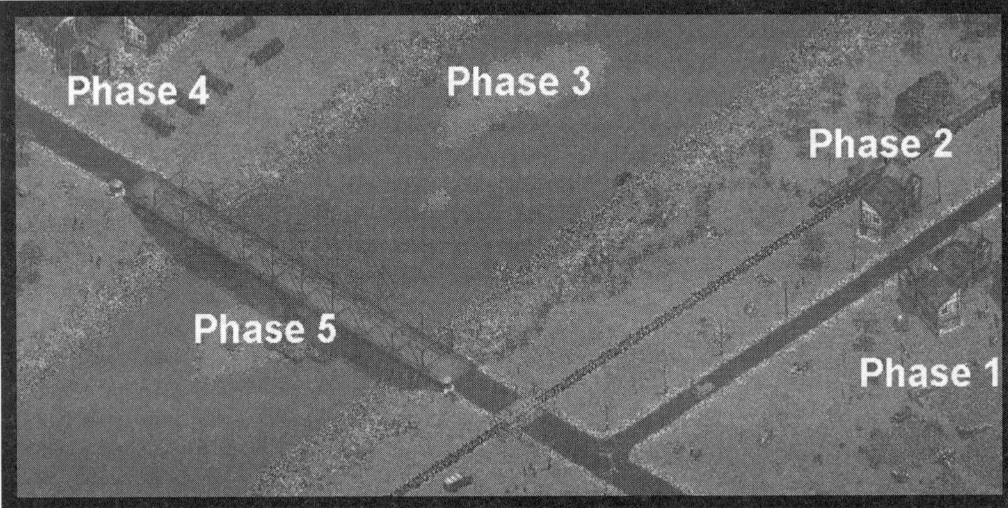

Figure 6-34. The Force of Circumstance

This long mission has your team traveling counterclockwise around the map. Your Commandos begin hidden in the fields in the southeast, surrounded by enemy soldiers.

The first phase is the most difficult: You must clear the area around the fields and destroy the barracks there. Then you must head north to secure the area around the train station and destroy that barracks, too. Next, you must secure the island in the northern part of the river as a landing spot for the subsequent assault on the German camp. There, steal a tank, and then clear the rest of the map. Finally, get the explosives and blow up the bridge before making your getaway.

PHASE 1: THE FIELDS

Again, this is the most difficult part of the mission. Your four Commandos are surrounded in the fields. A careless movement from your hiding spots and you could be caught.

Begin by dropping everybody prone. Then select the Sapper. When Soldier 1 heads away from you, sneak around the wall and place the trap there next to the wall. Watch out for Soldier 2: he has a good view to your advance to this position. If you don't place the trap close enough to the wall, other soldiers may spot Soldier 1's body. After you place it, crawl back to the hiding spot. Soldier 1 will walk into the trap and die unseen.

EUROPE

Figure 6-35. The beginning of the mission is the most difficult part: you're surrounded.

The Green Beret is next. After Soldier 3 comes toward him and turns around, have him move in an arc, first north and then west to the wall near Soldier 2, careful to stay out of his view. Before you get to the wall, move in, kill 2, carry the body to the wall, and drop it in the corner. Wait for Soldier 3 to return and walk past you. Quickly kill him and hide the body in the same place. Now, keeping an eye on patrols 6 and 7, sneak up and kill Soldier 4 and drop the body in the corner of the northern wall. As both patrols move away from you, run after and kill Soldier 5 in the courtyard; quickly move the body to the corner where 4 lies.

TIP

The corner of a wall or building is the best place to hide dead bodies and live Commandos. During this mission and many others you'll want to drop the bodies as quickly as possible and hide. To save time and place a body right in the corner, move your Commando directly into the corner and press C to drop prone. The Commando will drop the body automatically as he falls prone, depositing it right in the corner.

Flex those big muscles and send the Green Beret to pick up the explosive barrel and place it next to the door of the barracks Patrol 6 is circling. Wait until the patrols just turn away from you; this way you can position the barrel and have enough time left to crawl behind the nearest wall. Send the other three Commandos to hide in the building near 5. When Patrol 6 walks past the barrel, shoot it with the pistol and it will blow up, taking patrol and barracks with it. A single soldier will come out of the building. Shoot him quickly, and then crawl back to the hiding place.

Patrol 7 and others will come to examine the rubble from the explosion. Just stay put and you'll be fine. Patrol 7 will return to its route. As it walks past the Commandos hidden in the courtyard, exit all three from the building, group them, and pull out their pistols. Before firing, make sure all three of your Commandos are

TIP

Grouping several Commandos can increase your firepower: it takes one Commando three shots to kill an enemy soldier, but three Commandos can kill an enemy with a single shot, because each time the group fires, they shoot three bullets—the minimum to kill a soldier. This tactic gives you a good chance to kill a patrol and take little or no damage.

within pistol range. If they aren't, close until all three can hit a given target. Fire once at each of the soldiers in the patrol to kill them quickly. Then return to the hiding spot.

PHASE 2: THE TRAIN STATION

After you kill Patrol 7, jump back into the building. Other soldiers, such as 8 and 9, may hear the shots and come to investigate. Take them out with pistols. While the

Figure 6-36. After you clear the east side of the tracks, throw a grenade at the train station/barracks. Now the Germans have no more reinforcements.

train is at the station, lure any remaining enemy soldiers on the east side of the tracks to their deaths, and then hide all your Commandos in the building near 8.

You needn't be quiet. In fact, fire shots to lure enemies to places where you can easily kill them. Kill Patrol 15 when you have the opportunity. Reinforcements will come out of the train station, which is also a barracks. Sneak the Sapper toward the station, using the train for cover, and throw a grenade at Soldier 14. Then quickly return to the building. This will kill 14 and 13, destroy the barracks, and kill any reinforcements on the platform. The blast also damages the tracks so the next train can't pass through the station.

NOTE

Don't worry if an alarm sends reinforcements pouring out of the train station. The grenade will kill them all. In fact, by the time you're ready to throw the grenade, several soldiers probably will have been run over by the train as they walked too close to the tracks.

Shoot Soldier 16 with a pistol, and then hide until things settle down. After all soldiers return to their posts, your Commandos must crawl up onto the platform via the stairs near the building where they're hiding. Watch for the half-track as you do this. Send the Green Beret to knife Soldier 17, and then 18. Finally, move all the Commandos to the river's edge and take a quick break.

PHASE 3: THE ISLAND BEACHHEAD

The Marine must don his diving gear and hit the water. Swim to the island in the north part of the river. Here you must capture the boat and clear out all the soldiers: this is where you'll land the other Commandos after you pick them up with the boat.

But first things first. Swim west of Soldier 19. When he turns away and while

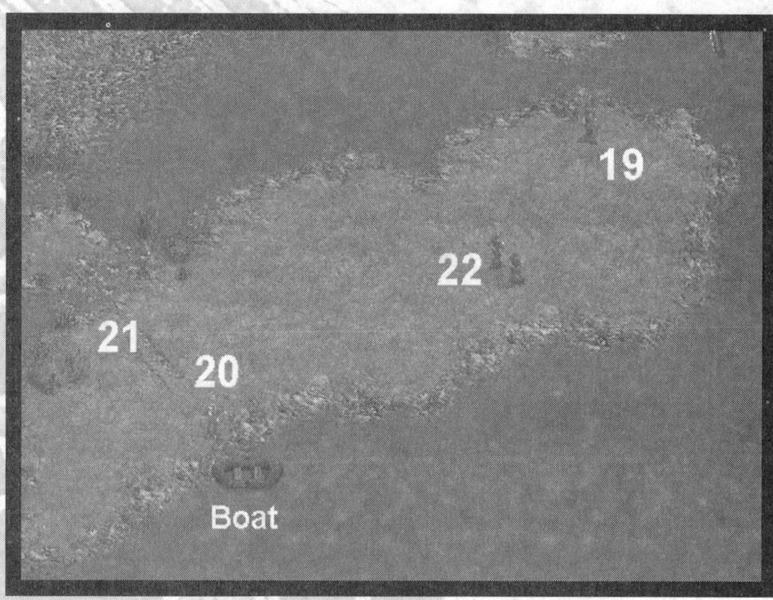

Figure 6-37. Have the Marine clear this island of all enemies so you can land the rest of the team.

the other soldiers aren't looking, pop out of the water, shoot him with the speargun, and then drop back below the surface. The other soldiers will see the body and cry for an alarm, but no one can hear them. Next, swim over near the boat, carefully kill Soldier 20, and drop back into the water. Repeat with 21, and then run after Patrol 22. While their backs are to you, kill the rearmost with the speargun; then pull out the pistol and shoot the next. Walk to the boat. Pick it up and put it in your knapsack; then run back into the water and swim to your waiting teammates.

PHASE 4: THE GERMAN CAMP

Patrol 23 will spot the dead soldiers on the island and go to investigate, so don't rush the Commandos there until after 23 leaves. You can carry only two passengers plus the Marine, who must row. Drop off the first two at the east edge of the island and go back for the third. Put the boat back in the knapsack before the Marine jumps into the water and swims downstream toward the bridge.

Carefully move the Sapper toward the German camp. Watch for Patrol 23. Wait for them to pass, and then move the Sniper toward the camp. Position him where you see the 'X' in figure 6-38. Wait for Patrol 23 to walk around the camp and head back toward you. Pull out your last grenade and throw it at the patrol as soon as they're in range. The blast will kill the patrol and Soldier 24. Drop

Figure 6-38. After you clear out the camp, the Driver can get to the tank. Then the fun begins.

prone and stay put. Several soldiers and patrols will come to investigate; however, they won't spot you behind the tent.

After the enemy returns to its normal activity, bring the Green Beret and Driver forward to where the Sapper is hiding. Move the Green Beret closer to Soldier 25, but out of sight of 26. When 26 turns away, run and kill 25 and carry the body back out of sight. Knife 26 when he turns his back on you again; hide his body, also. Approach Soldier 27 from the northwest and give him the blade. You can leave this body where it falls. Soldier 28 is a little tougher to get. You must place the decoy a little north of his tent and activate it. He'll run over to it, giving the Green Beret the opportunity for the kill. Hide the body and recover the decoy.

Now the Driver can crawl over to where the Green Beret waits. Before they continue, the Marine has a quick assignment: Swim upriver, even with and directly behind Soldier 29. Crawl up the bank and shoot him with the speargun when no one's looking at him. Drop prone and crawl back into the river. Have the Green Beret wait until the half-track drives west off the map. Then he must crawl up to

Soldier 30 and knife him as Soldier 31 turns to head north. Drop prone and crawl after 31. Kill him, and then bring the Driver up to climb aboard the tank along with the Green Beret.

PHASE 5: BLOW THE BRIDGE

As soon as the Driver is in control of the tank, fire at the half-track and the pillbox. Then continue shooting at all the enemies remaining on the west side of the river. Drive to the river's edge and fire at the machine-gun nest and soldiers on the island under the bridge. Return to the road and drive across the bridge, guns a-blazing. Kill all enemies on the other side of the river, including the half-track and pillbox. Take care not to destroy the truck—it's your ticket out.

When you've killed all the enemies on the map, the Marine can inflate the boat and row the Sapper to the island under the bridge to recover the explosives. Row to the eastern shore and disembark. While the other Commandos congregate near the truck, the Sapper must run onto the bridge and place the explosives. Position them at the brown "explosive" symbols. (Figure 6-39 shows them as A, B, and C.)

Return to the other Commandos and then detonate the explosives. Make sure the bridge is destroyed; then get everyone aboard the truck. With the Driver at the wheel, head down the road to the south map edge and safety.

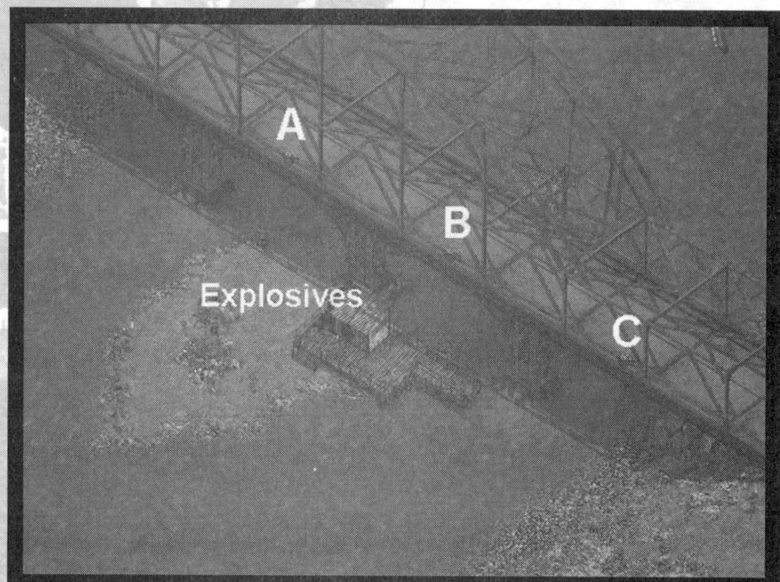

Figure 6-39.
The explosives lie on the little island below the bridge. Place the charges at A, B, and C, at the little "explosive" symbols.

MISSION 19: FRUSTRATE RETALIATION

GERMANY, JANUARY 12, 1945

While all of France is being liberated, the Soviets reach a devastated Warsaw. Berlin is the next stop for the Red Army. Meanwhile, the Germans begin launching V2 missiles—last hope of the Führer—against London and other Allied targets.

Reconnaissance flights have spotted a V2 launch center in a small industrial setting at Oldenburg, west of Bremen. You must destroy the launch pads before they launch missiles against London.

MISSION SUMMARY

Objective: Destroy all three V2 rockets and their launch pads.

Team: Green Beret, Sniper, Marine, Sapper

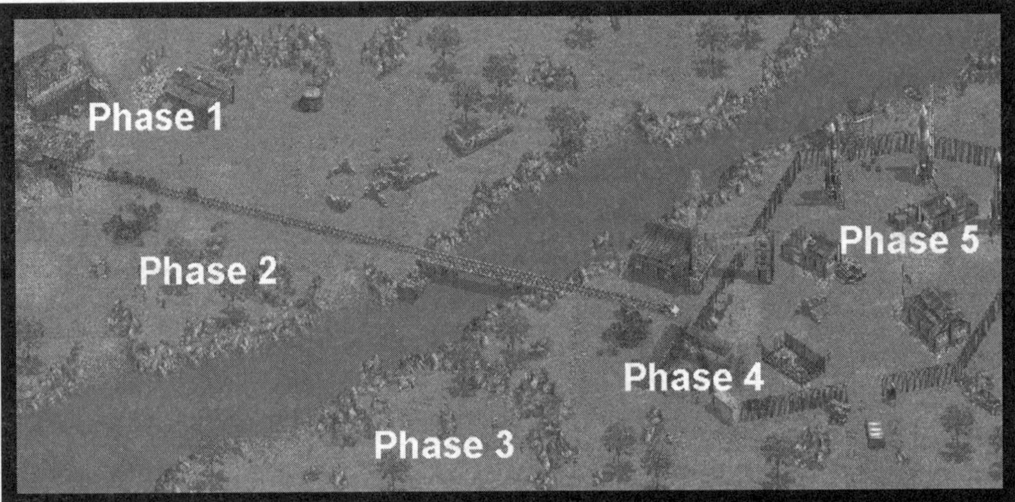

Figure 6-40. Frustrate Retaliation

This mission is fraught with danger for your Commandos. You must be skilled in controlling your men. They begin along the northern map edge. First, they must clear the area around the coal mine of enemy soldiers. Next, they must secure the area down by the river.

Send the Marine across the river to take out the small group of soldiers in the southwest and move all the Commandos across the bridge to the east side of the river. You must find a way into the base and clear it out so you can prepare to blow up the V2 missiles and their launchers, take out the barracks while you're there, and then make your way to the boat in the northeast and escape.

PHASE 1: THE COAL MINE

The Commandos begin along the northern map edge, near a tank shed and a bunker. There are many enemies on this side of the river, but you need only kill two-thirds of them. Many of the kills during this phase require good timing. The Green Beret starts off the show by running after Soldier 1 and killing him behind the rock as 2 walks away. Move the body to the start hiding place when the coast is clear again.

Now place the decoy west of the rock and lure Soldier 2 in for the kill. Hide his body, as well. Recover the decoy and place it near the north side of the shed containing the tank. Send the Sniper around the corner to shoot Soldier 3 atop the mine

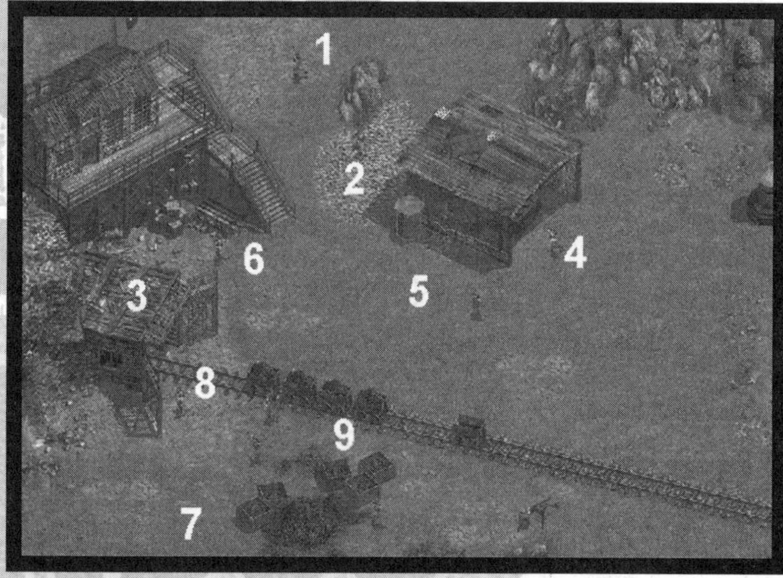

Figure 6-41.
The coal mine is crawling with enemy soldiers. You'll have to use cunning and deception to kill them all.

when no one's looking in his direction. Drop prone and crawl back to the hiding spot. Then the Green Beret can activate the decoy while he hides behind the rock near 2. Wait until Soldier 5 is walking away to attract only 4. Kill him, hide the body, and return to the rock. Activate the decoy again and 5 meets his death the same way.

NOTE

Beware of the tank in the shed. It looks shut down, but the crew is paying attention. If you move in front of it, prepare to die: it will fire its machine gun at your Commandos. The tank leaves the shed when the alarm sounds.

Now the Green Beret can move the decoy north of Soldier 6. Hide behind the rock, activate the decoy, and kill 6 when he comes to take a look. Move the Sapper to the mining office and place the trap at the foot of the stairs. Hide behind the rock while the Green Beret moves 6's body northeast of the trap and into Soldier 7's line of sight. He'll spot the body, come to investigate, and walk right into the trap and die. The Green Beret must quickly move the body out of sight while the Sapper recovers his trap.

Bring the Marine up to fight. Crawl to the coal cars near 8. Wait until 9 turns away and kill 8 with the speargun. Quickly run after 9, but hide in the little gap in the coal. As 9 passes on his way to 8's body, shoot him with the speargun, as well. Then have the Green Beret hide the bodies.

PHASE 2: CLEARING THE PATH TO THE BRIDGE

To lure Soldier 10 to his death, the Green Beret must place the decoy in between the coal and the coal cars. Hide in the coal and activate the decoy. Soldier 10 will come around to see what's making such a racket. Knife him as he walks past, and then hide

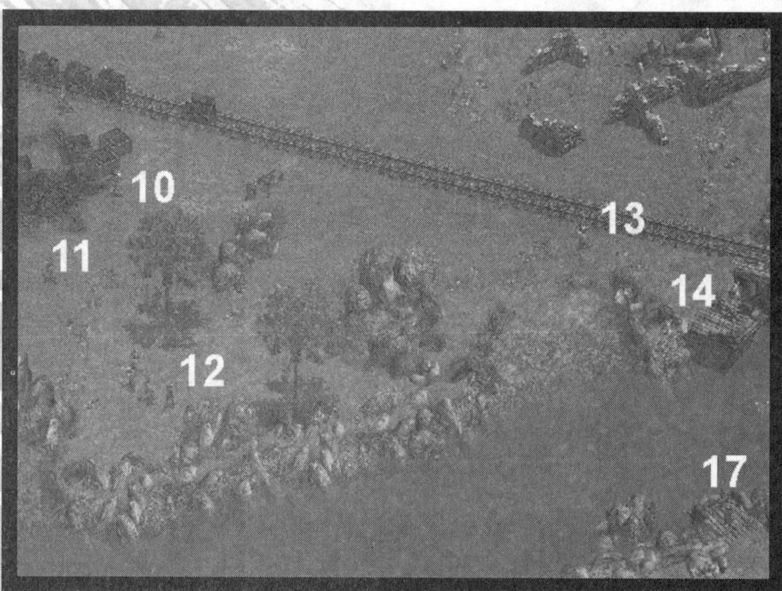

Figure 6-42.
You must kill a patrol, a machine-gunner, and a few soldiers to clear a path to the bridge.

the body in the coal. Now place the decoy in the coal, as well. Move your Commandos to the other side of the coal cars and activate the noisemaker. Soldier 11 will walk your way. When he's past the spot where 8 stood guard, run after and kill the curious enemy. Hide his body in the coal. Retrieve the decoy.

Carefully move all your Commandos to the western map edge and down to the river. Leave the Sniper along the western edge. He must shoot all four soldiers in Patrol 12 without allowing them to raise an alarm. Kill them as they begin walking east so their bodies will fall out of view of 13. Because the Sniper must shoot as quickly as he can, don't bother dropping prone after each shot. You may have to make several tries to time it right. Once the patrol is history, however, move the Sniper down to join his friends.

The Green Beret can crawl over to the patrol's bodies and move one into 13's field of view. Then run east to hide behind the rock. As 13 comes to see what's happened, knife him and hide his body near the rock.

Now have the Marine don his diving gear and hop into the river. Swim downstream to the bank by Machine-gunner 14. When Soldier 17 looks away, get out of the water and immediately hit the dirt. Crawl behind 14 and shoot him with the speargun when 17 again looks elsewhere. Drop prone as fast as you can, and then return to the river.

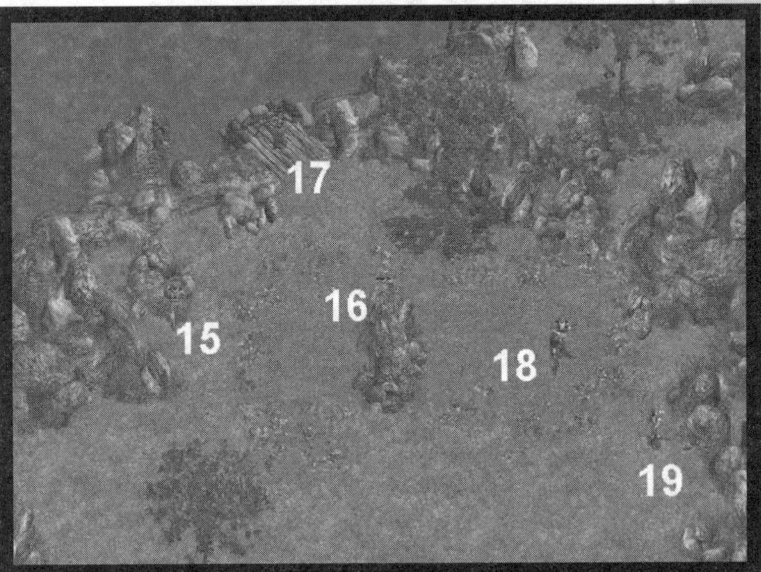

Figure 6-43. Before your Commandos can cross the river safely, the Marine must take out the machine gun on the opposite side, along with its supporting soldiers.

PHASE 3: DOWN BY THE RIVER

Swim the Marine to the bank on the southwest side of the river and crawl out. You must kill all these soldiers single-handedly. While keeping an eye on 18, sneak over near 15. When 18 heads south, run and shoot 15 with the speargun when his back is turned. You must kill him before he reaches the end of his route, where 16 can see him. Crawl over to 16 and knife him when 18 moves south again. Quickly run over and shoot Machine-gunner 17 with the speargun and return to hiding near 16. Run after Patrol 18 on its southern route; kill the soldier, and then the dog, with the speargun. Finally, kill Soldier 19 silently and return to the river. Swim back across and join the rest of the team.

PHASE 4: GETTING INTO THE BASE

Group your Commandos and crawl across the bridge and into the building on the other side. Have the Sapper plant a remote-control explosive in the middle of the bridge. When Soldier 20 turns and heads south, the Green Beret must exit the build-

Figure 6-44. Sneak your Commandos into the base using the conveyor belt.

ing, run after 20 and knife him. Carry the body around to the other side of the coal to hide it. Bring out the Sapper, now, and move him and the Green Beret to the edge of the conveyor belt, out of sight of soldiers 21 and 22. When both head away from you, the Green Beret must run after 21, kill him, and hide the body behind the rock.

The Sapper should join him when it's safe to do so. Then, while 22 heads east, the Sapper must place the trap in his path, behind the concrete wall. Return to the rock and wait for 22 to die. While this is going on, move the Sniper to the rock. After 22's demise, the Sniper must crawl along the southern map edge until he has a shot at the dog in the cage. Unless the dog dies, it will bark and alert the soldiers to your presence.

Now the Green Beret is ready to scale the wall. Wait until both 25 and 29 walk away from you before climbing. At the bottom, hide behind the rocks to the west. Kill 24 with the knife (when 25 walks away again) and carry the body to the door of the dog cage. Next, sneak up behind 25 and give him the cold, hard steel, as well. Dump his body near 24's.

Crawl over to the flashing switch and click on it once. The conveyor belt will reverse directions. The other three Commandos need only crawl onto it to travel into the base. Have the Green Beret pull out his decoy and place it northwest of 26. Hide south of the wall and activate it. Soldier 26 will walk around so

you can kill him easily. Hide the body west of the wall, and then use the same procedure on 27.

PHASE 5: DESTROY THE V2S

When Soldier 29 heads north on his route around the barracks, move the Green Beret and Marine over behind 28. Knife this soldier, and then carry the body toward the south corner of the building, so 32 won't see it. Then the Marine must shoot 29 with the speargun as he comes around the corner. Move his body near 28's and send the Marine back to join the others.

Now the Green Beret can kill Soldier 30 when Patrol 36 heads north. Hide the body behind the crates west of the gate.

Before moving into the northern part of the base, where you might be seen from across the river, have the Sapper blow the bridge. This will set off an alarm—but the alarm will be across the river. No one in the base will know what's happened.

Move the Green Beret to the building north of 26 while the other three hide in

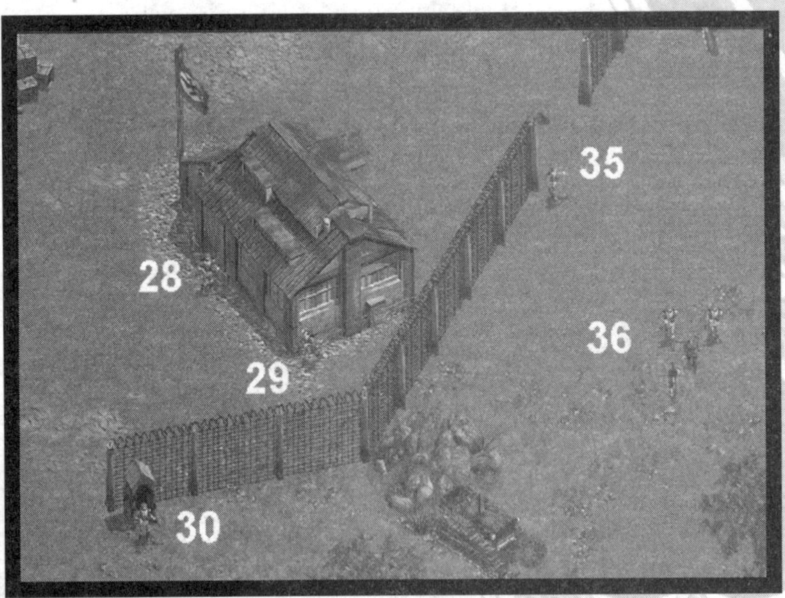

Figure 6-45. Clear the area around the southern barracks.

Figure 6-46.
You must kill all the soldiers on the base before you can blow up the missiles.

the tall, narrow building nearby. Place the decoy near the building's door. Both soldiers 31 and 32 hear it and stop in their tracks. However, you won't lure them. Instead, use this to alter the timing of their routes. Shut the decoy off, and then run after 31 to kill him when both turn back around. Carry the body to the western corner of the building. Then, during 32's next walk away from you, run after and knife him. Hide the body behind the center V2.

Now the Sniper can leave cover and crawl north to the space between the western two missiles. He needs a shot to kill 33 near the eastern map edge. When this is accomplished, the Sniper can return to join the other two Commandos.

TIP

You may be tempted to use the Sapper's second explosive on a barracks, but keep it in his knapsack. You'll need it for the watchtower during your getaway.

Now hide the Green Beret behind the eastern V2. Wait until Patrol 36 heads south, and then kill Soldier 34. Carry the body to the west side of the south barracks. It's also a good idea to kill 35 and hide his body when the patrol isn't looking.

It's time to set up the explosives. There are four barrels near the watchtower. Place one next to each missile and near the west corner of the south barracks. Place one barrel between the eastern V2 and the north barracks to take both out. Position the Green Beret north of this barrel near the fence, and the Marine west of the southern barracks.

The Marine can fire first. After the explosion, drop prone. A single soldier walks out from the flames. Kill him, and then crawl to a building. The Green Beret must shoot his barrel as quickly as you can switch over to him. By now, some troops may have come out. When you hit the barrel, you'll kill them all *and* take out the barracks and the V2. Patrol 36 will run into the base. Just stay out of their sight and destroy the other two V2s. When the patrol returns to its post, send all your Commandos out of the base through the south gate.

Run west around the fence, and then head north. After passing the building, drop prone and crawl. Send the Sapper ahead to plant the explosive under the watch tower. He must move quickly and carefully so the guards above won't spot him. Move back from the tower and blow it up.

Now get all your Commandos into the boat. The Marine can row them downstream to safety. Mission accomplished.

MISSION 20: OPERATION VALHALLA

FRANCE, FEBRUARY 11, 1945

The Soviet Army has entered East Prussia. The Third Reich's end seems imminent. Suddenly, a secret teletype casts a shadow over the confident Allied command: detailed technical plans of Fat Man, the first nuclear bomb developed by the Manhattan Project, have been stolen by a Nazi spy and taken across the Atlantic to Gundelfingen Castle, north of Freiburg. From there, they'll be taken to an underground secret base somewhere in the Carpathian Mountains, where a German atom bomb is in the final stages of development. You must enter the castle and put an end to this terrible threat.

MISSION SUMMARY

Objective: Blow up the headquarters in Gundelfingen Castle, as well as both V2 missiles.

Team: Green Beret, Sniper, Marine, Sapper, Driver, Spy

This is *COMMANDOS'* most difficult mission. The castle is filled to the brim with enemy soldiers. Just getting all your Commandos into the fortress will be tough. The Green Beret must lead the way and provide access for the Marine and the Spy. The three will work together from there to get the other three in, as well. You must clear a path to both the headquarters and the tank. Don't waste time killing enemies who are out of your way.

EUROPE

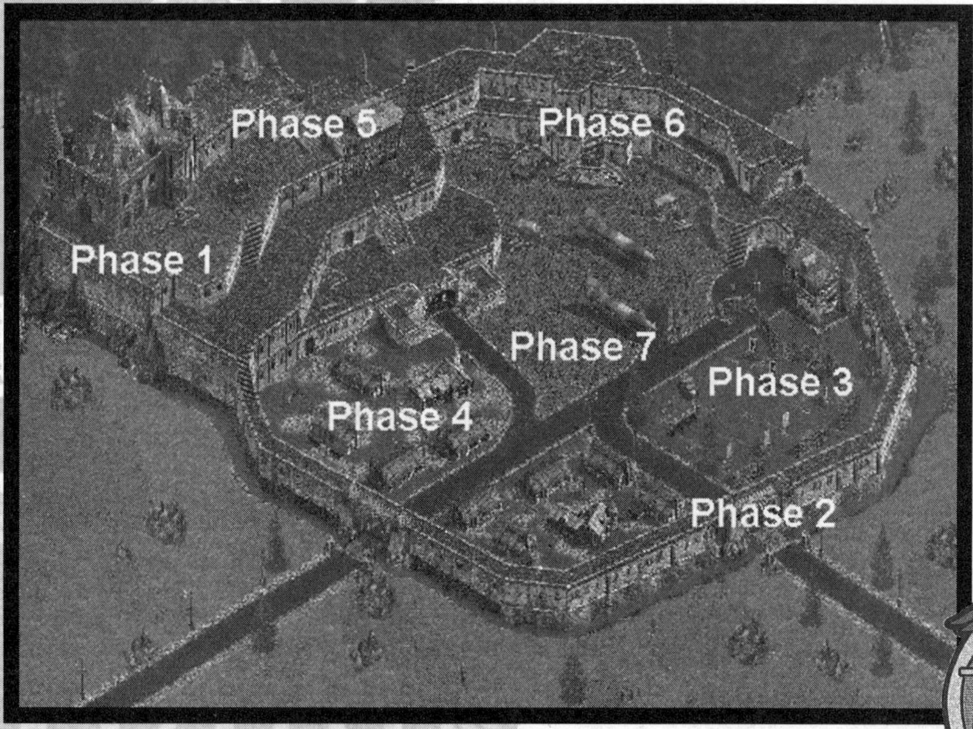

Figure 6-47. Operation Valhalla

This mission is very picky about the order in which you kill the soldiers. Kill some, and the alarm immediately goes off; kill others, and there's no reaction whatever. Almost every soldier can be seen by one or more of the other soldiers. Always make sure you're in the clear before taking any action in this mission walkthrough. Good luck.

PHASE 1: OVER THE WALL

Your Commandos begin separated: the Green Beret and the Spy are in the west, while the Sniper, Marine, Sapper, and Driver are in the east. Because four soldiers guard each gate into the castle, you must find an alternative route. The Green Beret is the only Commando able to scale vertical faces, so he gets the job.

Crawl to the west wall below the headquarters and begin climbing. You want to clear the top as Soldier 1 walks west. If it doesn't look like this will happen, click the cursor below and then above you to make the Commando go up and down until the coast is clear. At the top, run after Soldier 1 and knife him. Kill Soldier 2, and then

Figure 6-48. The Green Beret must scale the castle's west wall and kill all soldiers along it.

climb the ladders and take out 3 atop the tower. Some of the soldiers below can see the tower, so make sure they're looking away when you pop up and knife the guy.

Climb back down the ladders, and then scale the interior wall near 2. Wait until 4 walks away before going over the edge. Run after and knife Soldier 4; then do the same to 5 and 6.

TIP

During this mission, crawl everywhere unless the text specifically recommends you run. More than a hundred eyes are looking for you, so take care.

PHASE 2: A STROLL AROUND THE OUTER WALL

The Green Beret must now crawl down the stairs and begin his trip around the outer wall. Crawl as close as possible to Soldier 7 without being seen; then, when he turns

Figure 6-49. The Green Beret must crawl all along the outer wall to the other side of the castle. Take out only those guards who could cause problems later.

around, pull out the knife and crawl after him as fast as your knees can go. If you time it right, you should be able to kill him just before he turns and spots you. Leave the body and continue.

Crawl behind the two soldiers at the south corner. If you try to kill them, you'll be spotted and probably killed. Either way, the alarm sounds and you'll have to start over at your last save. Kill Soldier 8 with the knife before you continue. Soldier 9 is in view of several soldiers in the firing range below, so make sure no one's looking before you slit his throat. Creep on toward 10. Wait at the periphery of his view, and then crawl quickly after him when he turns away. Finally, kill Soldier 11, and then move over near the ladder down into the firing range.

TIP

While crawling around the walls, don't move along the interior of the wall or the soldiers below may spot you. Instead, keep to the center of the path.

PHASE 3: THE FIRING RANGE

The firing range, with its high concentration of soldiers, is a tough area. The Green Beret must climb down the ladder as Soldier 13 moves east and when 18 isn't looking. Quickly kill 12, and then run after and kill 13 and 14. Hide all the bodies in the corner by the ladder. It's time for some help.

Move over to the switch and open the water gate. Now the Marine can enter the water outside the wall and, using his diving gear, swim under the wall and into the castle. Crawl the Marine to Soldier 15 and kill him with the speargun when 19 is checking his target. Soldier 16 will see the body and come over to be speared as well. The Green Beret must move both bodies out of sight before they're seen.

Figure 6-50.
The firing range is the only area where you can use pistols without automatically setting off alarms.

Next, place the decoy behind Soldier 17. Activate it once the Green Beret is in the corner near the ladder. When 17 looks toward the sound, the Marine can sneak behind and shoot him with the speargun. Quickly return to cover, because 18 and 19 see the body and come to take a look. Depending on which soldier comes first and what path he takes, use the Green Beret and Marine as a team, with each killing the soldier who walk into their sights. Avoid using the pistols unless absolutely necessary. If one of your Commandos is caught, freeze and quickly send the other one over to kill the enemy soldier before he can shoot or sound an alarm.

TIP

Although you can fire a pistol in the firing range area without alerting the rest of the castle, the soldiers in the area will notice that the shots didn't come from the right place and will come looking for you, possibly even sounding the alarm. Therefore, avoid using the pistol unless absolutely necessary, or if the walkthrough recommends otherwise.

You must kill one more soldier before moving on to the next phase. While lying near 15's post, the Marine should fire a shot into the air with his pistol. Quickly crawl over to the spring and hide underwater. Soldier 20 will come to investigate the shot. When he goes to return to his post, rise out of the water and go after him with the speargun. Have the Green Beret hide the body in the usual spot. Next, carefully crawl out onto the firing range and place the decoy behind Soldier 21 so the soldier across the street from him won't see your crawling Commando. Move the Green Beret along the wall to the southeast gate. Activate the decoy and run across the road and hide behind the building on the other side. You must act quickly: Soldier 21 won't be distracted long. Also, this trick will only work once, so do it right the first time.

PHASE 4: ENTER THE SPY

Now the Green Beret must make his way unseen along the wall to the other gate. You must time your movements carefully, so the soldiers in this southern corner of the castle won't suspect your presence. In fact, you don't have to kill anyone here until the very last phase.

Figure 6-51. Once the Spy gets the uniform, he can use it to clear this area of enemy soldiers.

Hide in the building at the south corner until Patrol 26 with four soldiers enters the southwest gate and goes down the road; then carefully crawl to hide near the next building, just across the street from Soldier 22 and still out of his sight. When he looks away from you, run across the street and into the gateway behind the rearmost soldiers of Sentry 25. Wait until 22 and 23 look away again, then knife 22 and move into the corner where 22 was standing before 23 sees you. Run after and kill 23 as 24 heads away from you. Hide the body in the alcove by the door. Knife 24 when you can and carry his body, as well as 22's, to join 23's. By now, Patrol 26 should be coming, so hide in the building until they pass. Then take out the gate guards one at a time, starting with the rear ones. Knife each and hide the body before killing the next to prevent a buildup of bodies you won't have time to move before the patrol comes around again. After you dispose of all the gate guards, and when none of the outside patrols is watching, get the Spy into the castle to join the Green Beret.

The Spy must get a uniform. (Of all missions, he chooses this one to not bring his!) You must time his movements perfectly to avoid being seen by soldiers 30 and 31. Crawl until the clothesline covers you; then, when no one's looking, run to the uniform and put it on. If your timing is just a little off, you'll be discovered.

Now send the Spy to distract the soldier across the street from 27 so the Green Beret can knife 27 and dispose of the body. Next, distract 31 so the Green Beret can kill 28. Move the Spy over to talk to 30 while the Green Beret knifes 29. Finally, the Spy can poison 30, 31, and 32 by himself. Leave the bodies where they lie. If you try to move them, you risk being caught.

Soldier 33, at the top of the castle, will spot 32's body and come down to investigate. Keep the Green Beret hidden in the building with the alcove while the Spy kills 33. Soldier 34 also comes down. Repeat the procedure on him, and then take a quick break.

PHASE 5: THE HEADQUARTERS

Now the Spy can walk all the way to the top of the castle. Poison Soldier 35 when 40 looks away. Then go over to do the same to 36. Kill both 37 and 38 before walking over to 39. Wait until 40 looks away before injecting the poison. As 40 tries to find out what happened to his friend, poison him quickly, or he'll call out for the alarm.

That's all you need to do at the headquarters. If you try to kill more soldiers, you'll be caught and killed. Move back down to the Green Beret and help him get back to the firing range by distracting enemies along the way. The Green Beret should wait by the building near the gate, hidden in the little corner. The Spy now must begin a conversation with Soldier 21 and distract his attention from

Figure 6-52. The Sapper is still outside the castle, so take this opportunity to clear a path for him to the headquarters.

the gate. Then the Green Beret can take out the gate guard and hide the bodies in the corner of the nearby building. Wait for Patrol 26 to pass through before beginning. You must kill both rear guards quickly before moving the bodies. You can take out the front guards one at a time, as you did at the other gate. With the gate cleared, bring in the remaining Commandos and move them all to hide near 15's post with the Marine.

PHASE 6: GET TO THE TANK

This phase is very tricky and requires a specific sequence of killings. The Green Beret should place the decoy near the barracks by the firing range. Activate it while hiding by the ladder. This lures Soldier 42 into the area—an easy kill for the Spy. Just make sure Patrol 57 isn't around. Hide the body by the ladder. Now the Spy can climb the stairs and kill Soldier 43 when 44 isn't watching. Climb to the next level and kill 44 as 45 walks away. Run toward 45 and poison him as he heads back to 44's body.

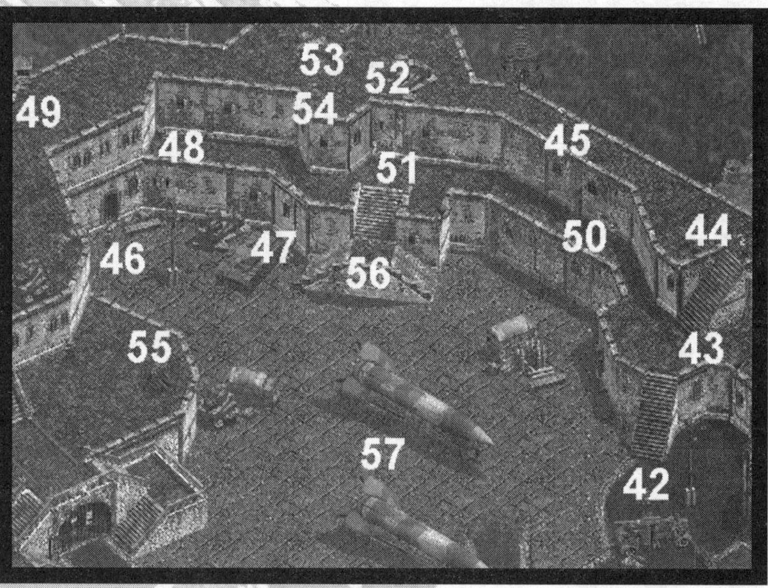

Figure 6-53.
You must kill the enemies surrounding the tank in a certain order to prevent an alarm from sounding.

TIP

This phase can be very frustrating. You'll probably be caught several times while you're in the process of killing. We recommend quicksaving after each kill to avoid having to eliminate the same soldiers again and again.

Now walk back down to ground level and poison soldiers 46, 47, and 48 when the coast is clear. Soldier 49, above, spots one of the bodies and decides to come down and have a look. Run over to the stairs by 32's post and kill 49 before he can cause trouble. While the Spy goes solo, the other Commandos should carefully climb the ladder and crawl along the wall to hide in the door by 43's post.

Send the Sapper along the top of the outer wall to plant his remote-control explosive next to the headquarters door. As long as you crawl, you'll be safe. Take care when crawling past the two soldiers on the wall in the south. After completing this assignment, return to the hiding place with the rest of the team.

The Spy needs the Green Beret's help in the next few killings. Knife 50

while the Spy distracts 51; then crawl over and kill 51, as well. Get both of them to the top level. The Spy must distract 54 and keep him looking south. The Green Beret must wait for 53 to walk north past 54 before killing 52. Then run after and kill 53 before he can turn around. Finally, knife 54. Be sure to drop prone after each kill, except when you have to run after 53.

Send the Green Beret back to the hiding place while the Sapper walks over to Soldier 56. Move the Sniper up the stairs to 44's post and pull out the precision rifle. Take aim at Gunner 55 with the antitank gun and shoot to kill. Quickly drop prone after the shot and return to join the others in hiding. It's finally time for the Driver to earn his pay. Order him to crawl along the second level over to where the Spy is waiting. When Patrol 57 heads south, poison Soldier 56 and get the Driver into the tank.

PHASE 7: ENDGAME

With the antitank gun out of action, nothing can stop the tank. Before moving (and alerting the enemy), exit the Sapper from the building so he can detonate his explosive and destroy the headquarters. Get him back inside so he doesn't get hurt. It's also a good idea for the Spy to ride in the tank, safe from all the coming destruction. The Driver should be sure to blow up both V2 missiles, and then shoot back at anything that fires at you. If you take out the barracks early on, you'll have fewer soldiers to deal with. Clear the eastern part of the castle, and then get the remaining Commandos aboard the tank. Drive out the southwest gate, down the road, and off the map to safety.

Congratulations. You've completed this mission—and the game!

CHAPTER 7

MULTIPLAYER MISSIONS

As with many of today's games, *Commandos* includes multiplayer capability. While most real-time strategy games pit players against each other, *Commandos* allows players to complete the missions cooperatively. Choose any of the 20 missions in the single-player campaign. Each player then receives one or more Commandos to control.

The keys to playing with other humans are communication and coordination. Choose one player to lead. The leader must make sure that everyone understands his or her responsibilities. At the beginning of a mission, the players should hold a brief planning session. Divide the mission into phases and assign each player appropriate roles. In several instances, players can complete tasks in different areas of the map at the same time. They also may cooperate to set up an ambush.

The walkthroughs' strategies and tactics apply to multiplayer missions as well. Having more than one Commando in action at a time dictates a few modifications. We include these here, as well as tables of suggested assignments, broken down by mission. In some missions, a Commando such as the Driver may have nothing to do until the end. The Sniper may play a limited role, because his ammunition is set at that beginning and he can't kill silently.

TIP

The host is responsible for saving the game. Save after each phase. If the players are working independently, they should notify the host when they complete their assignments. When someone makes a mistake, everyone must start over at the last save.

MISSION 1: BAPTISM OF FIRE

SUGGESTED ASSIGNMENTS

Number of Players	Green Beret	Marine	Driver
2	PLAYER 1	PLAYER 2	PLAYER 1

This quick and easy mission is a good one for trying your hand at multiplayer. While the Marine gets the boat, the Green Beret and Driver can be making their way to the dock. Once on the northern island, the Marine can kill the machine-gunner, while the Driver takes control of the machine gun to kill the patrol before they know what's happening.

Figure 7-1.
Blow up the relay station on the northern island.

MISSION 2: A QUIET BLOW-UP

SUGGESTED ASSIGNMENTS

Number of Players	Green Beret	Sniper	Marine	Sapper	Driver
2	PLAYER 1	PLAYER 1	PLAYER 2	PLAYER 2	PLAYER 2
3	PLAYER 1	PLAYER 2	PLAYER 3	PLAYER 2	PLAYER 2
4	PLAYER 1	PLAYER 2	PLAYER 3	PLAYER 4	PLAYER 2

Figure 7-2.
You must destroy the depot inside the walled compound.

The Green Beret, the Marine, and the Sapper can all take part in clearing the east side of the river. After the Marine takes them across the river and the Green Beret lowers the ladder, each Commando has his own task. The Driver readies the truck while the Green Beret and Sniper kill the two guards. Then the Sapper must place the explosives. The Marine is just there for the ride home.

MISSION 3: REVERSE ENGINEERING

SUGGESTED ASSIGNMENTS

Number of Players	Green Beret	Marine	Sapper	Spy
2	PLAYER 1	PLAYER 1	PLAYER 2	PLAYER 2
3	PLAYER 1	PLAYER 2	PLAYER 3	PLAYER 3

Figure 7-3.
You must blow up the dam and then escape.

The Marine does most of the killing in the camp, the Green Beret does it in the power plant, and the Spy distracts soldiers. The Sapper cuts through the fence and takes care of the explosives.

MISSION 4: RESTORE PRIDE

SUGGESTED ASSIGNMENTS

Number of Players	Green Beret	Sniper	Marine	Sapper	Driver
2	PLAYER 1	PLAYER 1	PLAYER 2	PLAYER 2	PLAYER 2
3	PLAYER 1	PLAYER 2	PLAYER 3	PLAYER 2	PLAYER 3
4	PLAYER 1	PLAYER 2	PLAYER 2	PLAYER 3	PLAYER 4

The Green Beret and Sapper must work together to clear out the western part of the map with a little help from the Marine. The Driver takes the tank and finishes up the area as well as clearing out a section across the fjord. Once across the bridge, the Sniper can take out his targets while the Green Beret clears the southeast and the Driver gets the machine gun and a truck. Once inside the yard of the head-

Figure 7-4.
You must destroy the German headquarters.

quarters, work as a team to kill all the soldiers there. Divide up your targets before the shooting starts.

MISSION 5: BLIND JUSTICE

SUGGESTED ASSIGNMENTS

Number of Players	Green Beret	Spy
2	PLAYER 1	PLAYER 2

This is a great two-player mission because both must work together closely to coordinate their actions and pull it off. Just follow the walkthrough.

Figure 7-5.
Blow up the radar at the mountaintop base and escape in the autogyro.

MISSION 6: MENACE OF THE LEOPOLD

SUGGESTED ASSIGNMENTS

Number of Players	Green Beret	Sniper	Sapper
2	PLAYER 1	PLAYER 2	PLAYER 2

The Green Beret does most of the killing while the Sniper and Sapper have only limited roles.

Figure 7-6.
Blow up the Leopold cannon.

MISSION 7: CHASE OF THE WOLVES

SUGGESTED ASSIGNMENTS

Number of Players	Green Beret	Marine	Sapper	Driver	Spy
2	PLAYER 1	PLAYER 1	PLAYER 2	PLAYER 2	PLAYER 2
3	PLAYER 1	PLAYER 2	PLAYER 3	PLAYER 3	PLAYER 3
4	PLAYER 1	PLAYER 2	PLAYER 3	PLAYER 3	PLAYER 4

This is an excellent mission for multiplayer. Because the Commandos are split into two teams, they can carry out their assignments simultaneously. They don't have to coordinate until near the end of the mission.

Figure 7-7.
You must sabotage the two U-boats while they're in dock.

MISSION 8: PYROTECHNICS

SUGGESTED ASSIGNMENTS

Number of Players	Green Beret	Sniper
2	PLAYER 1	PLAYER 2

This mission goes more smoothly with two players, but the Sniper has a very limited role. However, he must be ready to act when the time comes.

Figure 7-8.
You must destroy all the water and fuel at this depot.

MISSION 9: COURTESY CALL

SUGGESTED ASSIGNMENTS

Number of Players	Green Beret	Sniper	Sapper	Driver	Spy
2	PLAYER 1	PLAYER 1	PLAYER 2	PLAYER 2	PLAYER 2
3	PLAYER 1	PLAYER 2	PLAYER 2	PLAYER 2	PLAYER 3
4	PLAYER 1	PLAYER 2	PLAYER 3	PLAYER 2	PLAYER 4

Figure 7-9.
Destroy the antenna, communications control building, weapons store, command post, and bunker.

This is another good multiplayer mission. After the base is cleared, each Commando plays a part in preparing to destroy the objectives. This mission is also short, which makes for a quick game.

MISSION 10: OPERATION ICARUS

SUGGESTED ASSIGNMENTS

Number of Players	Green Beret	Sniper	Sapper	Driver
2	PLAYER 1	PLAYER 2	PLAYER 1	PLAYER 2
3	PLAYER 1	PLAYER 2	PLAYER 3	PLAYER 2

Assign the pilot to the player controlling the Sniper. At the final phase, the Sapper and Driver will have their hands full taking out enemy tanks as fast as they can. Until then, however, the Green Beret does most of the killing.

Figure 7-10.
You must rescue the downed pilot and destroy the weapons store.

MISSION 11: IN THE SOUP

SUGGESTED ASSIGNMENTS

Number of Players	Green Beret	Sniper	Sapper	Driver	Spy
2	PLAYER 1	PLAYER 1	PLAYER 2	PLAYER 1	PLAYER 2
3	PLAYER 1	PLAYER 2	PLAYER 2	PLAYER 2	PLAYER 3
4	PLAYER 1	PLAYER 2	PLAYER 3	PLAYER 2	PLAYER 4

Figure 7-11.
You must destroy all four oil rigs.

The Green Beret and the Spy must work closely. The other Commandos must support these two during their assignments. The Sapper places explosives and traps while the Driver takes control of a half-track and mows down enemy soldiers with the machine gun.

MISSION 12: UP ON THE ROOF

SUGGESTED ASSIGNMENTS

Number of Players	Green Beret	Sniper	Spy
2	PLAYER 1	PLAYER 1	PLAYER 2

This mission requires a lot of coordination between the Spy and the Green Beret. For two players, give the Informer to the Spy. Have the Sniper take care of him when there are three players.

Figure 7-12.
You must rescue the Informer and get all your men out of town.

MISSION 13: DAVID AND GOLIATH

SUGGESTED ASSIGNMENTS

Number of Players	Green Beret	Sniper	Marine	Sapper	Driver
2	PLAYER 1	PLAYER 1	PLAYER 2	PLAYER 2	PLAYER 1
3	PLAYER 1	PLAYER 2	PLAYER 3	PLAYER 2	PLAYER 2
4	PLAYER 1	PLAYER 2	PLAYER 3	PLAYER 4	PLAYER 4

Figure 7-13.
You must sink the *Bismarck II* and blow up the fuel tanks.

The Green Beret and Marine can do much of their early killing simultaneously. Toward the end, the Sniper and Marine must coordinate a shot at Soldier 13.Remember, the timing is critical.

MULTIPLAYER

MISSION 14: D-DAY KICKOFF

SUGGESTED ASSIGNMENTS

NUMBER OF PLAYERS	GREEN BERET	SNIPER	MARINE	SAPPER	DRIVER
2	PLAYER 1	PLAYER 1	PLAYER 2	PLAYER 2	PLAYER 2
3	PLAYER 1	PLAYER 2	PLAYER 3	PLAYER 2	PLAYER 2
4	PLAYER 1	PLAYER 2	PLAYER 3	PLAYER 4	PLAYER 2

This mission requires a lot of coordination between the Green Beret and the other Commandos. The Driver does nothing until the end, when he drives the tank and clears out the entire map.

Figure 7-14.
You must destroy the four gun emplacements.

MISSION 15: THE END OF THE BUTCHER

SUGGESTED ASSIGNMENTS

NUMBER OF PLAYERS	SNIPER	MARINE	DRIVER	SPY
2	PLAYER 1	PLAYER 1	PLAYER 2	PLAYER 2
3	PLAYER 1	PLAYER 2	PLAYER 2	PLAYER 3

Figure 7-15.
You must kill the SS general and blow up the headquarters building.

The spy does most of the work during the first part of the mission. He only distracts patrols at the end. The Sniper actually plays a major role during the last few phases.

MISSION 16: STOP WILDFIRE

SUGGESTED ASSIGNMENTS

NUMBER OF PLAYERS	SNIPER	MARINE	SPY
2	PLAYER 1	PLAYER 1	PLAYER 2

Figure 7-16. Prevent the bridge from being destroyed.

The phase where you kill all the Sappers at the same time makes this a great three-player mission. However, because the Marine doesn't do much, it's also great for two players.

MISSION 17: BEFORE DAWN

SUGGESTED ASSIGNMENTS

Number of Players	Green Beret	Marine	Spy
2	PLAYER 1	PLAYER 1	PLAYER 2

The Spy does most of the killing in this mission, so let the Marine control the prisoners. The Spy and the Green Beret must coordinate their actions, or the mission could end in disaster.

Figure 7-17.
Rescue the imprisoned French Resistance soldiers.

MISSION 18: THE FORCE OF CIRCUMSTANCE

SUGGESTED ASSIGNMENTS

Number of Players	Green Beret	Marine	Sapper	Driver
2	PLAYER 1	PLAYER 2	PLAYER 2	PLAYER 1
3	PLAYER 1	PLAYER 2	PLAYER 2	PLAYER 3

Figure 7-18.
You must now blow up the bridge you protected earlier.

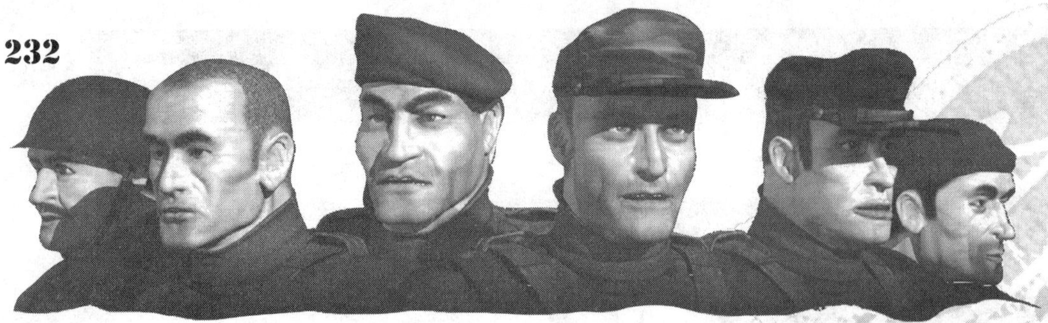

Assign roles according to the groups you'll need at the end, rather than the beginning. The Green Beret does most of the early killing, while the Driver mops up with the tank.

MISSION 19: FRUSTRATE RETALIATION

SUGGESTED ASSIGNMENTS

Number of Players	Green Beret	Sniper	Marine	Sapper
2	PLAYER 1	PLAYER 1	PLAYER 2	PLAYER 2
3	PLAYER 1	PLAYER 2	PLAYER 3	PLAYER 2

Both the Marine and the Green Beret do a lot of killing in this mission, but the Sniper and Sapper are also busy. The Sapper should watch the bridge and detonate the explosive just as enemy troops walk across. When it comes time to shoot the barrels, having the Green Beret and Marine controlled separately is a big help.

Figure 7-19. You must destroy all three V2 missiles and their launch pads.

MISSION 20: OPERATION VALHALLA

SUGGESTED ASSIGNMENTS

NUMBER OF PLAYERS	GREEN BERET	SNIPER	MARINE	SAPPER	DRIVER	SPY
2	PLAYER 1	PLAYER 1	PLAYER 2	PLAYER 1	PLAYER 2	PLAYER 2
3	PLAYER 1	PLAYER 2	PLAYER 2	PLAYER 1	PLAYER 3	PLAYER 3
4	PLAYER 1	PLAYER 2	PLAYER 3	PLAYER 3	PLAYER 2	PLAYER 4
5	PLAYER 1	PLAYER 2	PLAYER 3	PLAYER 2	PLAYER 4	PLAYER 5

This monster mission is a great one for multiplayer. For most of the mission, however, only the Green Beret, the Marine, and the Spy get to do anything. It's the only mission that allows for six players, which means a lot of coordinating and communicating.

Figure 7-20.
You must destroy the depot inside the walled compound.

APPENDIX

INTERVIEW WITH EIDOS

I had the terrific opportunity to work with *COMMANDOS* producer Eric Adams, from Eidos, on the production of this strategy guide. He granted me an interview about the game's development and plans for the future. Eric even included a few tips for game success.

Q: What inspired *COMMANDOS*?

A: *COMMANDOS* was inspired by exploits of real WWII Commandos and classic Hollywood WWII films. In creating *COMMANDOS* as a computer game, we wanted to break new ground. We wanted a real-time tactical game with strategic, puzzle-solving, and RPG elements. We wanted to give users the whole gameplay package.

Q: When did work begin on *COMMANDOS*?

A: Work began in February 1997. Javier Perez and his brother Ignacio Perez created Pyro Studios in Madrid, Spain. Javier also manages the leading Spanish distributor of PC and console games. Pyro approached Eidos Interactive with proposals for three games. We chose *COMMANDOS*.

Q: How did the game evolve?

A: *COMMANDOS* was always going to be real-time. There were issues on how to present its characters. We wanted to present an intimate group of men at your control, not cardboard cutouts.

A major issue was Commando mortality: When Commandos were killed, should we allow resurrection in the next mission or make the player restart? There were valid arguments for both methods. We chose the latter, because it fit the game's underlying theme of strong, specialized characters that are both your tools and your friends in this epic struggle. Just as in the *A-Team*, if you lose a main character, not only is the mission a bust, but so is the series.

There were plans for including rotatable cameras. However, during playtesting we found that the traditional isometric camera was fine. We invested the time in gameplay balancing.

Multiplayer gameplay went through several variations. We finally decided the game engine worked best for cooperative multiplayer gaming. A humans–vs.–computer-Germans game was more in the *COMMANDOS* spirit. We also enhanced the multiplayer game's look and functionality.

Q: Why did you choose real-time over turn-based?

A: At first there was some concern, because tactical wargamers often are vehemently split on the type of action they want. We didn't want to alienate a segment. In the end, I think real-time was the only way to go. *COMMANDOS* is a small-scale battle of wits. It proceeds at a pace that's manageable and allows for planning. However, we do have moments of intense combat action.

Q: Who's your favorite Commando?

A: Pyro loves Tiny McHale, the Green Beret. I like Fins, the Marine, and Sid, the Driver. Each Commando has endearing qualities that users can appreciate.

Q: Did you model any of the men on actual people?

A: The Commando characters were modeled after real Commandos and their combat roles. We also used the film *The Dirty Dozen* as a character study. Tiny was modeled after Charles Bronson, with a smidgen of Rambo added in.

Q: Which movies inspired certain missions?

A: Movies that inspired us include *The Dirty Dozen, Force Ten from Navarone, Where Eagles Dare,* and *The Great Escape.* We wanted to capture the flavor and excitement of these epic films, and give players a crack at emulating their movie heroes.

Q: Are you planning a sequel or add-on missions?

A: We're planning both. *COMMANDOS* is an international hit. *COMMANDOS* will have a sequel and add-on disk that will advance the original to new heights of graphical brilliance and intriguing gameplay.

Q: What are some other Pyro Studios games, and what are their future plans?

A: This is Pyro Studios' first game. They plan a mission add-on disk for Christmas. *COMMANDOS II* is coming next year. The tentative plan is for a Pacific theater theme. There's a good probability of a console port of *COMMANDOS II.* Be assured, the "dirty half-dozen" will be back in action. We plan to listen to users *very* carefully and incorporate their ideas and demands into the sequel.

Q: Can you offer any favorite tactics or tips?

A: My favorite tactic is grouping your Commandos behind an obstruction, alerting the guards, and then ambushing them as they come around the corner. You can really deplete garrison forces that way.

Here are some other tips:

1. Always conserve Duke's ammo. Only use the precision rifle on distant sentries overlooking strategic locations.
2. If Inferno (the Sapper) has extra time bombs, blow up a garrison to eliminate the threat of reinforcements quickly.
3. Always heal your men before the mission ends. Wounded Commandos count against your score.

Q: Which mission is your favorite, and why?

A: My favorite mission is Mission 15, "End of the Butcher." Assassinating an evil Nazi general in a heavily guarded Parisian city is both cinematic in scope and devilishly hard in execution. Escaping in the graveyard is classic. As always, when you complete a mission, there's an incredible sense of accomplishment. In this case, not only is the general dead, but your French colleagues are safe.

Game designer Ignacio Perez's favorite is Mission 20, "Operation Valhalla." I don't want to give too much away, but this mission defines "tension."

Q: Will you release an editor so players can create their own missions?

A: There's a lot of demand for an editor. At this time, however, the editor is designed only as a development tool for Pyro designers. With the plan calling for so many *COMMANDOS* products, it's doubtful we'll release one.

INDEX

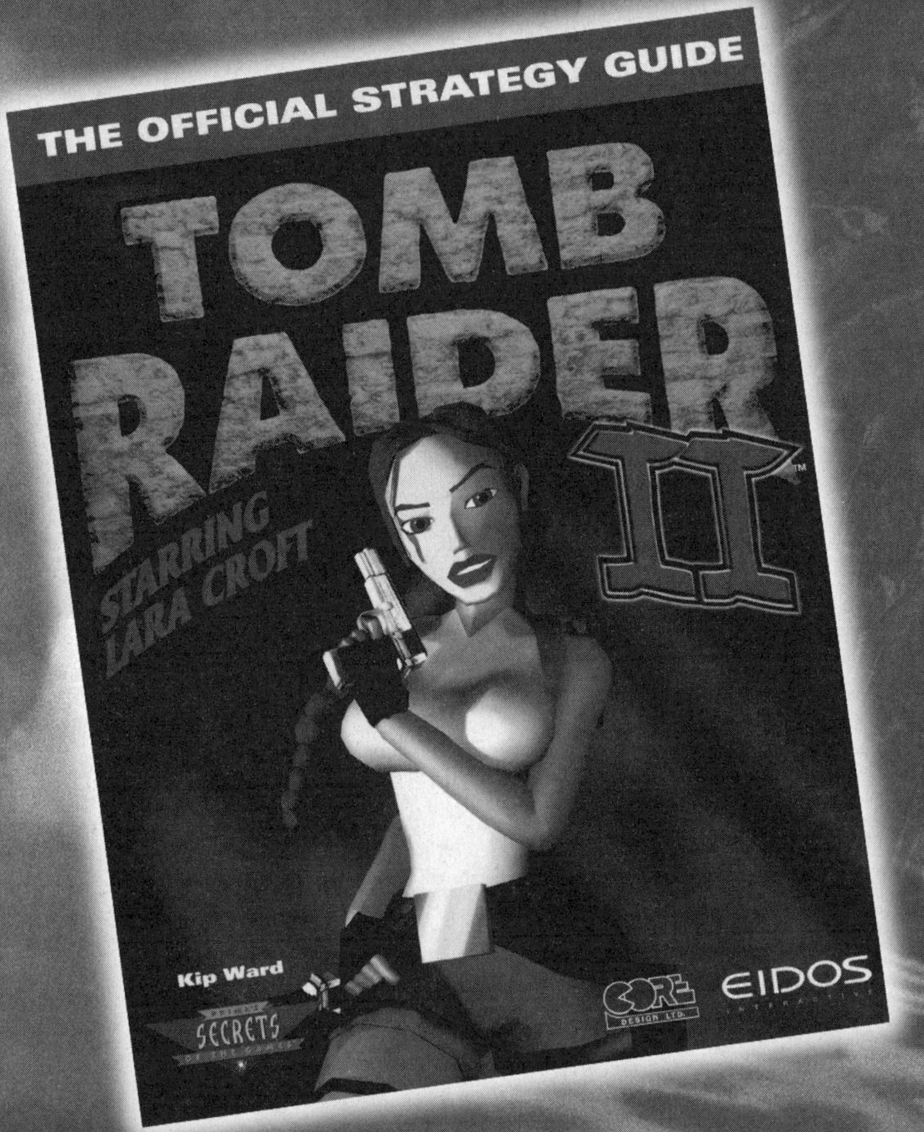
THE OFFICIAL STRATEGY GUIDE
TOMB RAIDER II
STARRING LARA CROFT
Kip Ward
SECRETS
CORE DESIGN LTD.
EIDOS

To Order Books

Please send me the following items:

Quantity	Title	Unit Price	Total
______	______________________	$ ______	$ ______
______	______________________	$ ______	$ ______
______	______________________	$ ______	$ ______
______	______________________	$ ______	$ ______
______	______________________	$ ______	$ ______

*Shipping and Handling depend on Subtotal.

Subtotal	Shipping/Handling
$0.00–$14.99	$3.00
$15.00–$29.99	$4.00
$30.00–$49.99	$6.00
$50.00–$99.99	$10.00
$100.00–$199.99	$13.50
$200.00+	Call for Quote

Foreign and all Priority Request orders: Call Order Entry department for price quote at 916-632-4400

This chart represents the total retail price of books only (before applicable discounts are taken).

Subtotal $ ______

Deduct 10% when ordering 3-5 books $ ______

7.25% Sales Tax (CA only) $ ______

8.25% Sales Tax (TN only) $ ______

5.0% Sales Tax (MD and IN only) $ ______

7.0% G.S.T. Tax (Canada only) $ ______

Shipping and Handling* $ ______

Total Order $ ______

By Telephone: With American Express, MC or Visa, call 800-632-8676 or 916-632-4400. Mon–Fri, 8:30-4:30.

www.primapublishing.com

By E-mail: sales@primapub.com

By Mail: Just fill out the information below and send with your remittance to:

Prima Publishing
P.O. Box 1260BK
Rocklin, CA 95677

My name is ______________________

I live at ______________________

City ______________________ State ______ ZIP ______

MC/Visa# ______________________ Exp. ______

Check/money order enclosed for $ ______________ Payable to Prima Publishing

Daytime telephone ______________________

Signature ______________________